First World War
and Army of Occupation
War Diary
France, Belgium and Germany

2 CAVALRY DIVISION
Divisional Troops
Signal Squadron Royal Engineers
1 August 1915 - 30 April 1919

WO95/1123/7

The Naval & Military Press Ltd
www.nmarchive.com
Published in association with The National Archives

Published by

The Naval & Military Press Ltd

Unit 10 Ridgewood Industrial Park,

Uckfield, East Sussex,

TN22 5QE England

Tel: +44 (0) 1825 749494

www.naval-military-press.com

www.nmarchive.com

This diary has been reprinted in facsimile from the original. Any imperfections are inevitably reproduced and the quality may fall short of modern type and cartographic standards.

Contents

Document type	Place/Title	Date From	Date To
Heading	WO95/1123/4		
Heading	1915-1919 2nd Cavalry Division 2nd Signal Squadn R.E. Aug 1915-Apl 1919.		
Heading	War Diary Of 2nd Signal Squadron August 1915 (Vol I). From 1st To 31st Aug 1915 To Apl 1919		
War Diary	Le Niepe	01/08/1915	04/08/1915
War Diary	Lemeppe-Roquetoire	06/08/1915	07/08/1915
War Diary	Roquetoire	08/08/1915	31/08/1915
Heading	2nd Cavalry Division 2nd Signal Squadron R.E Vol II Sept 15		
War Diary	Roquetoire	01/09/1915	23/09/1915
War Diary	Roquetoire Monchy Cayeux	24/09/1915	24/09/1915
War Diary	Monchy-Cayeux	25/09/1915	25/09/1915
War Diary	Lozinghem	25/09/1915	27/09/1915
War Diary	Maries-Lez-Mines	27/09/1915	29/09/1915
War Diary	Ferfay Ecqyeburvod	29/09/1915	30/09/1915
Heading	2nd Cavalry Division 2nd Signal Squadron R.E Vol III Oct 15		
War Diary	Ecquedecques	01/10/1915	03/10/1915
War Diary	Ham-En-Artois	03/10/1915	16/10/1915
War Diary	Roquetoire	17/10/1915	19/10/1915
War Diary	Thiembronne	20/10/1915	31/10/1915
Heading	War Diary Of 2nd Sig Sqdn R.E Period Nov 1915		
War Diary	Thiembronne	01/11/1915	30/11/1915
Heading	2nd Signal Sqn (2nd Cav Div) Dec 1915 Vol V		
War Diary	Thiembronne	01/12/1915	31/12/1915
Heading	2nd Signal Sqn Jan 1915 Vol VI		
War Diary	Thiembronne	01/01/1916	05/05/1916
War Diary	Lumbres	06/05/1916	22/06/1916
War Diary	Hazebrouk	22/06/1916	30/06/1916
Heading	War Diary Of 2nd Signal Squadron. R.E. from 1st July To 31st July 1916 (Volume XXIII)		
War Diary	Hazebrouck	01/07/1916	31/07/1916
Heading	War Diary Of 2nd Signal Squadron For August, 1916. Vol 13		
War Diary	Hazebruck	01/08/1916	31/08/1916
Heading	War Diary Of 2nd Signal Squadron For September, 1916. Volume 13		
War Diary	Hazebrouck	01/09/1916	06/09/1916
War Diary	St. Venant	06/09/1915	06/09/1915
War Diary	Monchy Cayeux	07/09/1916	07/09/1916
War Diary	Williman	08/09/1916	09/09/1916
War Diary	Frohen Le Grand	10/09/1916	10/09/1916
War Diary	Vignacourt	11/09/1916	12/09/1916
War Diary	Lahoussoye	12/09/1916	14/09/1916
War Diary	L3d 6.5	15/09/1916	28/09/1916
War Diary	F2 A C 6.4	29/09/1916	30/09/1916
Diagram etc			
Diagram etc	2nd C.D Cct Diagram		
Diagram etc	Appendix IV		

Diagram etc	2nd Cavalry Division Circuits		
Diagram etc	2nd C.D Cct Diagram		
Diagram etc	2nd Cav Div Circuits		
Diagram etc	2nd Cav Divn Ccts		
Heading	War Diary Of 2nd Signal Squadron, R.E. October, 1916. Vol 15		
War Diary	F24 C6.4 (albrust Sheet)	01/10/1916	06/10/1916
War Diary	F24c 6.4	07/10/1916	31/10/1916
Diagram etc	App I		
Diagram etc	2nd Cav Div Circuits		
Heading	War Diary Of 2nd Signal Squadron, R.E. Novermber 1916. Vol. XXVII.		
War Diary	F24.c 6.4	01/11/1916	02/11/1916
War Diary	E28.b.9.9	03/11/1916	11/11/1916
War Diary	Ligescourt	11/11/1916	30/11/1916
Diagram etc	2nd Cav Division Cct Diagram		
Diagram etc	2nd Cav Divn Cct Diagram		
Diagram etc	2nd Cav Div Circuit Diagram		
Diagram etc	2nd Cavalry Division Circuit Diagram		
Heading	War Diary Of 2nd Signal Squadron, R.E. December, 1916. Vol. XXVIII.		
War Diary	Ligescourt	01/12/1916	31/12/1916
Heading	War Diary Of 2nd Signal Squadron, R.E. January, 1917 Vol. XXIX.		
War Diary	Ligescourt	01/01/1917	31/01/1917
Heading	War Diary Of 2nd Signal Squadron, R.E. February 1917. Vol. XXX		
War Diary	Ligescourt	01/02/1917	28/02/1917
Heading	War Diary Of 2nd Signal Squadron, R.E. March, 1917. Vol. XXXI.		
War Diary	Ligescourt	01/03/1917	31/03/1917
Heading	War Diary Of 2nd Signal Squadron, R.E. April, 1917. Vol. XXXII.		
War Diary	Ligescourt	01/04/1917	06/04/1917
War Diary	Chateau De Beauvoin	07/04/1917	07/04/1917
War Diary	Henu	08/04/1917	09/04/1917
War Diary	Agny	09/04/1917	12/04/1917
War Diary	Henu	13/04/1917	30/04/1917
Heading	War Diary Of 2nd Signal Squadron, R.E. Vol. XXXIII. May, 1917.		
War Diary	Frohem Le Grande	01/05/1917	11/05/1917
War Diary	St Ouen	12/05/1917	12/05/1917
War Diary	Bussy Les Daours	13/05/1917	13/05/1917
War Diary	Lamotte En Santerre	14/05/1917	14/05/1917
War Diary	K.10.c.a8.	15/05/1917	18/05/1917
War Diary	K.11.A.7.9	19/05/1917	31/05/1917
Heading	War Diary Of 2nd Signal Squadron, R.E. From 1/6/17 To 30/6/17 Volume XXXIV		
War Diary	K.11.a.7.9	01/06/1917	30/06/1917
Heading	War Diary Of 2nd Signal Squadron, R.E. From 1st July To 31st July 1917 Volume XXXV		
War Diary	K.11.a.7.9.	01/07/1917	09/07/1917
War Diary	Courcelles	09/07/1917	16/07/1917
War Diary	Hoovin	17/07/1917	31/07/1917
Heading	War Diary Of 2nd Signal Squadron, R.E. From 1/8/17 To 31/8/17 Volume XXXVI		

War Diary	Houvin-Houvigheul	01/08/1917	31/08/1917
Heading	War Diary Of 2nd Signal Squadron, R.E. From September 1st 1917 To September 30th 1917 Volume XXXVII		
War Diary	Houvin Houvisneul	01/09/1917	30/09/1917
Heading	War Diary Of 2nd Signal Squadron, R.E. From 1/10/17 To 31/10/17 Vol No. XXXVIII		
War Diary	Houvin	01/10/1917	01/10/1917
War Diary	Houvigneul	02/10/1917	07/10/1917
War Diary	Heuchin	08/10/1917	22/10/1917
War Diary	St. Sauflieu	22/10/1917	31/10/1917
Heading	War Diary Of 2nd Signal Squadron, R.E. From 1/11/17 To 30/11/17 Vol No. XXXIX		
War Diary	St-Sauflieu	01/11/1917	17/11/1917
War Diary	Monchy Lagache	18/11/1917	26/11/1917
War Diary	Fins	27/11/1917	30/11/1917
Heading	War Diary Of 2nd Signal Squadron, R.E. From 1st December 1917 To 31st December 1917 Volume XL		
War Diary	Fins	01/12/1917	10/12/1917
War Diary	Quevauvillers	11/12/1917	31/12/1917
Heading	War Diary Of 2nd Signal Squadron, R.E. From 1/1/18 To 31/1/18 Vol No. XLI		
War Diary	Quevauvillers	01/01/1918	31/01/1918
Heading	War Diary Of 2nd Signal Squadron, R.E. From Feb 1st 1918 To Feb 28th 1918 Vol No. XLII		
War Diary	Quevauvillers	01/02/1918	05/02/1918
War Diary	Athies	06/02/1918	28/02/1918
Heading	War Diary Of 2nd Signal Squadron, R.E From 1/3/18 To 31/3/18 Vol XLIII		
War Diary	Athies	01/03/1918	13/03/1918
War Diary	Quesmy	13/03/1918	26/03/1918
War Diary	Chiry	27/03/1918	31/03/1918
Heading	War Diary Of 2nd Signal Squadron, R.E. From 1/4/18 To 30/4/18 Vol No. XLIV		
War Diary		01/04/1918	01/04/1918
War Diary	Gentelles	02/04/1918	02/04/1918
War Diary	Boves Rivery	03/04/1918	11/04/1918
War Diary	Auxi-Le-Chateau	12/04/1918	15/04/1918
War Diary	Blaringhem	15/04/1918	30/04/1918
Heading	War Diary Of 2nd Signal Squadron, R.E. From 1st May 1918 To 31st May 1918 Vol. No. XLV		
War Diary	Coyecque	01/05/1918	11/05/1918
War Diary	Montcavrel	11/05/1918	31/05/1918
Heading	War Diary Of 2nd Signal Squadron, R.E. From 1-6-18 To 30-6-18 Vol No XLVI		
War Diary	Montcavrel	01/06/1918	30/06/1918
Heading	War Diary Of 2nd Signal Squadron, R.E. From 1-7-18 To 31-7-18. Volume No. XLVIII.		
War Diary	Montcavrel	01/07/1918	13/07/1918
War Diary	Wail	14/07/1918	14/07/1918
War Diary	Le Cauroy	15/07/1918	21/07/1918
War Diary	Wail	22/07/1918	22/07/1918
War Diary	Montcavrel	23/07/1918	31/07/1918
Heading	War Diary Of 2nd Signal Squadron, R.E. From 1-8-18 To 31-8-18 Volume XLVIII		
War Diary	Montcavrel	01/08/1918	07/08/1918

War Diary	Longeau	08/08/1918	09/08/1918
War Diary	NW Of Warvillers	10/08/1918	31/08/1918
Heading	War Diary Of 2nd Signal Squadron, R.E. From 1-9-18 To 30-9-18 Vol No. XLIX		
War Diary	Grenas	01/09/1918	30/09/1918
Heading	War Diary Of 2nd Signal Squadron, R.E. From 1-10-18 To 31-10-18 Vol No. L		
War Diary	Grenas	01/10/1918	31/10/1918
Heading	War Diary Of 2nd Signal Squadron, R.E. From 1/11/18 To 30/11/18 Vol No. LI		
War Diary	Grenas	01/11/1918	06/11/1918
War Diary	Cambrai	07/11/1918	14/11/1918
War Diary	Maubeuge	15/11/1918	17/11/1918
War Diary	Thuin	18/11/1918	18/11/1918
War Diary	Morialme	19/11/1918	21/11/1918
War Diary	Bouvignes	22/11/1918	22/11/1918
War Diary	Leignon	23/11/1918	23/11/1918
War Diary	Marche	24/11/1918	30/11/1918
Heading	War Diary Of 2nd Signal Squadron, R.E. From 1/12/18 To 31/12/18 Vol No. LII		
War Diary	Marche	01/12/1918	16/12/1918
War Diary	Theux	17/12/1918	31/12/1918
Heading	War Diary Of 2nd Signal Squadron, R.E. From 1st To 28th February 1919 Volume LIV		
War Diary	Theux	01/02/1919	28/02/1919
Heading	War Diary Of 2nd Signal Sqdn. R.E. From. 1/3/19 to 31/3/19 (Volume LV.)		
War Diary	Theux	01/03/1919	10/03/1919
War Diary	Heagy Verviers)	11/03/1919	30/03/1919
Heading	War Diary Of 2nd Signal Squadron, RE. From 1/4/19 to 30/4/19 Volume LVII		
War Diary	Heusy (Verviers)	01/04/1919	30/04/1919

1915-1919

2ND CAVALRY DIVISION

2ND SIGNAL SQUADN R.E.

AUG 1915-APL 1919

2nd Cavalry Division

121/6550

CONFIDENTIAL.

WAR DIARY

OF

2nd SIGNAL SQUADRON.

August. 1915.

(VOL. I.)

From 1st to 31st Aug. 1915

to Apl 1919

Ref. Map. HAZEBROUCK 5a 1/100000

Instructions regarding War Diaries and Intelligence Summaries are contained in F. S. Regs., Part II. and the Staff Manual respectively. Title pages will be prepared in manuscript.

WAR DIARY
or
~~INTELLIGENCE SUMMARY.~~
(Erase heading not required.)

2nd SIGNAL SQUADRON No. Vol. I Date August 1915 2nd CAVALRY DIVISION

Army Form C. 2118.

Hour, Date, Place	Summary of Events and Information	Remarks and references to Appendices
LE NIEPPE.		
Sunday. August 1st.	Divisional H.Q. in billets at LE NIEPPE.	
Monday. August 2nd.	Officers accompanied by linemen reconnoitring ~~billeting~~ routes for communications in new billeting area.	
Tuesday. August 3rd.	Working party of 2 officers and 8 men laid D.5 cable air line to connect up 3 Cav Bde with Div. H.Q. in new area – from St ANDRE FM. (2' S.W. of A in AIRE) via St QUENTIN, MOULIN LE COMTE, & RINCQ to ROQUETOIRE CHATEAU. Time taken about 8 hours including building. This line was built part of the way on poles carrying civil power mains and though the cable was never within 12 feet of the power lines induction was extremely strong and violent shocks were obtained. It was therefore decided to rebuild portions next day.	
Wednesday. August 3rd.	Rebuilt this line so as to be inch clear of power poles everywhere. Induction still slightly felt.	
Thursday. August 4th.	Reeled up certain local lines – lines of Supply Column in HAZEBROUCK etc. Another party leading in new lines into ROQUETOIRE CHATEAU. A third party proceeded by motor lorry to VOLKERINCKHOVE and reeled up cable and wire from that place to LE LONG CHAMP cross roads. 3. C.B. [illegible]	

(9 29 6) W 2794 100,000 8/14 H W V Forms/C. 2118/11.

[illegible] Capt.

Instructions regarding War Diaries and Intelligence Summaries are contained in F. S. Regs., Part II. and the Staff Manual respectively. Title pages will be prepared in manuscript.

WAR DIARY
or
~~INTELLIGENCE SUMMARY.~~
(*Erase heading not required.*)

2nd SIGNAL SQUADRON No. Vol. I Date August 1915 2nd CAVALRY DIVISION

Army Form C. 2118.

Hour, Date, Place	Summary of Events and Information	Remarks and references to Appendices
1915		
Friday. August 6th. LE NIEPPE — ROQUETOIRE.	The Remainder of the Division moved to the new billeting area. Divl: HQ at ROQUETOIRE CHATEAU. 3. CB ST ANDRÉ FM. 4 CB. to LE NIEPPE. 5. CB to BLARINGHEM.	
	Report centre closed at LE NIEPPE at 10-am and reopened at ROQUETOIRE CHAu same hour.	
	Remainder of day spent arranging and organizing new communications.	
	The want of sufficient motor transport is much felt during all moves – as it is difficult to lay new lines & reel up old ones quickly and at long distances unless a motor lorry is available to convey the working parties and stores.	
	During this move motor lorries were borrowed with very successful results – the new lines being all laid by the time units arrived in their new areas.	
Saturday. August 7th.	Rigged derricks for lead in of new lines – completed work in Signal Office – installed telephone exchange. Completed local lines etc –	

[signature] Capt.

(9 29 6) W 2794 100,000 8/14 H W V Forms/C. 2118/11.

Instructions regarding War Diaries and Intelligence Summaries are contained in F. S. Regs., Part II. and the Staff Manual respectively. Title pages will be prepared in manuscript.

WAR DIARY
~~or~~
~~INTELLIGENCE~~ SUMMARY.
(*Erase heading not required.*)

2nd SIGNAL SQUADRON No. Vol. I Date. August 1915 2nd CAVALRY DIVISION

Army Form C. 2118.

Hour, Date, Place	Summary of Events and Information	Remarks and references to Appendices
ROQUETOIRE, 1915		
Sunday. August 8th.	Rest day.	
Monday. August 9th.	Reeled up spare cable etc. left by other units in vicinity, cleaning out billets. Arranging garage for motors etc.	
Tuesday August 10th. Wednesday. August 11th.	Overhauling and repairing D.S. cable. Soldering all joints. Signallers under instruction in linemens duties.	
Thursday August 12. Friday. August 13.	Signallers under instruction in visual Signalling and pair work.	
Saturday. August 14th.	Buzzer reading. Weekly inspection of Rifles. Smoke helmets. Field dressings etc.	
Sunday. August 15.	Church parade CAUCHIE D'ECQUES.	
Monday August 16.	Laid cable line round chateau grounds for use for practice in locating faults and line maintenance.	
Tuesday. August 17. Wednesday August 18. Thursday August 19.	Buzzer reading practice daily. Signallers under instruction with linemen during daily line patrols, and also on the test line laid for the purpose on 16th.	
Friday August 20.	Organizing and arranging distribution and method of carrying equipment and stores to meet varying circumstances.	

(9 29 6) W 2794 100,000 8/14 H W V Forms/C. 2118/11.

[illegible signature]

Army Form C. 2118.

Instructions regarding War Diaries and Intelligence Summaries are contained in F. S. Regs., Part II. and the Staff Manual respectively. Title pages will be prepared in manuscript.

WAR DIARY
or
INTELLIGENCE SUMMARY.
(Erase heading not required.)

2nd SIGNAL SQUADRON
No. VOL I
Date August 1915
2nd CAVALRY DIVISION

Hour, Date, Place	Summary of Events and Information	Remarks and references to Appendices
ROQUETOIRE 1915		
Saturday. August 21st.	Weekly inspection of arms – Smoke helmets – Field dressings etc –	
Sunday. August 22nd.	Church Parade Cauchie d'Ecques. 11.15. am. The day was the first clear fine one for almost 10 days – we have had thunderstorms and rain almost daily for a fortnight.	
Monday. August 23rd.	Signallers instruction. Buzzer reading and locating faults on line.	
Tuesday August 24. / Wednesday August 25th.	Visual Signalling. Helio. Flag. & Lamp reading (lamp by day and night)	
Thursday. August 26.	Visual Signalling. Station work.	
Friday August 27.	Route march. Active service order. via BLARINGHEM – LINDE – LE NIEPPE – WARDRECQUES. Lamp reading by night.	
Saturday August 28.	Usual Weekly inspections.	
Sunday. August 29.	Captain JOURDAIN Telegraph Officer of X French Army came over with O.C. Signals Cav: Corps. to inspect our office etc... He was shown the Signal Office – method of carrying stores and distribution – and visual signalling. Flag reading at 3½ miles and lamp by daylight at 1000 yds.	
Monday August 30.	Lecture on airline work and instruction in same.	
Tuesday August 31.	Overhauling and repairing cable.	[illegible] Capt. 21 Lancers Cmdg Signals 2 Cav Div 1/9/15

(9 29 6) W 2794 100,000 8/14 H W V Forms/C. 2118/11.

2nd Cavalry Division

121/7145.

2nd Signal Squadron RE.

Vol II

Sept 15

Instructions regarding War Diaries and Intelligence Summaries are contained in F. S. Regs., Part II. and the Staff Manual respectively. Title pages will be prepared in manuscript.

WAR DIARY

or

~~INTELLIGENCE~~ SUMMARY.

(~~Erase heading not required.~~)

Army Form C. 2118.

2nd SIGNAL SQUADRON · No. .... Date .... · 2nd CAVALRY DIVISION

Hour, Date, Place		Summary of Events and Information	Remarks and references to Appendices
ROQUETOIRE.	1915.		
Wednesday.	September 1st.	Visual Signalling. Overhauling Cables.	
Thursday.	September 2nd.	The Squadron attended a demonstration by gas expert from G H Q.	
Friday	September 3rd.	Visual reading tests. Helio. Flag. Lamp and Buzzer.	
Saturday.	September 4th.	Usual weekly inspections.	
Sunday.	September 5th.	Church parade etc.	
Monday.	September 6th.	Aircraft dropping messages at "Divisional Report Centre" from 1000 and 1500 feet.	
Tuesday.	September 7th.	Visual signalling and buzzer work.	
Wednesday.	September 8th.	Squadron marched at 4.30 am to WISQUES to take part in Cav. Corps Intercommunication Scheme – the object being to test and practice :– (a). Intercommunication between Corps & Division over ground impassable for wheels. (b). Intercommunication between cavalry & aircraft by wireless and dropped messages and also by actual landing of aeroplanes. (c). Lateral communication between divisions. (d). Encyphering and decyphering ~~aeroplane~~ messages (e). Use of code with aeroplanes. Many lessons were learnt from this scheme.	S.M.B. Capt.

(9 29 6) W 2794 100,000 8/14 H W V Forms/C. 2118/11.

Instructions regarding War Diaries and Intelligence Summaries are contained in F. S. Regs., Part II. and the Staff Manual respectively. Title pages will be prepared in manuscript.

WAR DIARY
or
INTELLIGENCE SUMMARY.
(Erase heading not required.)

2nd SIGNAL SQUADRON
No.
Date
2nd CAVALRY DIVISION

Army Form C. 2118.

Hour, Date, Place	Summary of Events and Information	Remarks and references to Appendices
ROQUETOIRE. 1915.		
	It was found.	
Wednesday. Sept: 8. (contd.)	1. Personnel of Signal Squadrons insufficient to provide visual communication to Corps – divisions on each flank – and also brigades of the division: and also provide mounted or cyclist dispatch riders as well. All the seven signallers were employed in visual signalling to Corps and divisions – none being available for dispatch riding – and none would have been available for forward communications to brigades.	
	2. Pigeons proved a reliable means of communication under these conditions.	
	3. Value of reports received by aeroplanes provided the system of wireless can be made reliable in working.	
	4. Time taken in cyphering and decyphering messages for wireless detracts much from the value of this means of communication.	
Thursday Sept. 9th.	Lamps reading at 2 miles distance.	
Friday. Sept. 10th.	A helio station was sent to MONT DES CATS and communication was established from the hill WSW of RACQUINGHEM to this station, a distance of 18 miles, in spite of considerable haze.	
Saturday. Sept. 11.	Usual weekly inspections.	[signature] Capt.

(9 29 6) W 2794 100,000 8/14 H W V Forms/C. 2118/11.

Instructions regarding War Diaries and Intelligence Summaries are contained in F. S. Regs., Part II. and the Staff Manual respectively. Title pages will be prepared in manuscript.

WAR DIARY
or
INTELLIGENCE SUMMARY.
(Erase heading not required.)

2nd SIGNAL SQUADRON * No........ Date........ 2nd CAVALRY DIVISION *

Army Form C. 2118.

Hour, Date, Place	Summary of Events and Information	Remarks and references to Appendices
ROQUETOIRE. 1915.		
Sunday. September 12th.	Church parade etc...	
Monday. September 13th.	Divisional Intercommunication scheme tests and practice.	
	(a). Intercommunication by visual signalling between division and Brigades - Brigades and regiments. and lateral communication. under circumstances where the use of wires would be impossible and orderlies dangerous; and opening communication with Stations in unknown positions.	
	(b). Intercommunication between divl: HQ. and aircraft - both by wireless and dropped messages.	
	(c). Communication between Corps HQ + Divl. HQ. by wireless. visual - and ~~aeroplanes~~ telephone.	
	(d). Use of pigeons for communication between Bdes + Corps + Divn. + Corps.	
	(e). Rapid laying of telephone cable.	
	(f). Communication by night by electric Lamps.	
	The day was favourable for visual and it worked extremely well.	
	As regards (d). The birds were sent up in baskets carried by mounted men and arrived rather battered by the jolting.	
		[illegible]. Capt.

(9 29 6) W 2791 100,000 8/14 H W V Forms/C. 2118/11.

Instructions regarding War Diaries and Intelligence Summaries are contained in F. S. Regs., Part II. and the Staff Manual respectively. Title pages will be prepared in manuscript.

WAR DIARY
or
INTELLIGENCE SUMMARY.
(Erase heading not required.)

2nd SIGNAL SQUADRON No. .... Date .... 2nd CAVALRY DIVISION

Army Form C. 2118.

Hour, Date, Place	Summary of Events and Information	Remarks and references to Appendices
ROQUETOIRE. 1915.		
Monday. Sept. 13th. (Contd).	As regards (f.) some lessons were learnt as to the present electric lamp especially. (1). The need for constant renewal of cells. (2). Great variation of results obtained with different lamps. (3). Great variation in focus in apparently identical lamps. (4). Certain defects in the lamp such as its great weight which renders it difficult to carry for a mtd. man or cyclist; the liability of internal connections to break loose in transport; excessive lateral range; and clumsy fittings for aligning.	
Tuesday. Sept. 14th.	Lecture to men on results of Monday's scheme. Practice in carrying verbal messages.	
Wednesday. Sept. 15th.	Conference of bde. and regtl. signalling officers on Monday's scheme, and organizing new system of "procedure" in visual signalling.	
Thursday. Sept. 16.	Instruction in laying and maintaining light enamelled telephone wire.	
Friday. Sept. 17th.	Cav: Corps: Signals scheme in the forenoon for practising cooperation of Cav: Signal Service and aircraft. Weather cloudy and unfavourable and aeroplane was unable to distinguish ground signals. Signallers dispatch riding scheme in conjunction.	[illegible] Capt.

(9 29 6) W 2794 100,000 8/14 H W V Forms/C. 2118/11.

Instructions regarding War Diaries and Intelligence Summaries are contained in F. S. Regs., Part II. and the Staff Manual respectively. Title pages will be prepared in manuscript.

WAR DIARY
or
~~INTELLIGENCE SUMMARY.~~
(Erase heading not required.)

2nd SIGNAL SQUADRON No. Date 2nd CAVALRY DIVISION

Army Form C. 2118.

Hour, Date, Place	Summary of Events and Information	Remarks and references to Appendices
1915.		
BORVETOIRE. Sat: 18th September.	Usual Saturday Routine.	
Sun: 19: September.	Church Parade etc –	
Mon: 20: September.	In the afternoon Cav: Corps Scheme – Cooperation of Cavalry and Aircraft.	
	Signor G. Marconi was present and inspected the apparatus.	
	5. pm. Conference of O.C.'s Signals and R.F.C. Wireless experts, on the subject	
	of Cooperation – intercommunication, ground signals, procedure etc –	
Tuesday. 21: Sept:	At 2. pm. The Bdes: of the Div: moved to an area to the South –	
	3. CB. about FEBVIN – PALFART. 4. CB. ERNY ST JULIEN. 5. CB. LIETTRES.	
	Div: Troops MAMETZ. Divl: HQ did not move.	
	Communication with all units in the Div: by Motor Cyclist d/r. with	
	"posts" 4 times a day. it not being worth while to lay cable line	
	for only 2 days.	
Wednesday. 22: Sept:	Repacking and redistributing Stores for maximum mobility of transport.	
	Handed in all surplus cable and spare stores.	
	After dark tested forms of all lamps at short and long distance.	
	It is found that each electric lamp has a certain individual difference	GHB Capt.
	in focus which needs careful noting.	

(9 29 6) W 2794 100,000 8/14 H W V Forms/C. 2118/11.

Instructions regarding War Diaries and Intelligence Summaries are contained in F. S. Regs., Part II. and the Staff Manual respectively. Title pages will be prepared in manuscript.

WAR DIARY
or
~~INTELLIGENCE SUMMARY.~~
(*Erase heading not required.*)

2nd SIGNAL SQUADRON No. .... Date .... 2nd CAVALRY DIVISION

Army Form C. 2118.

Hour, Date, Place	Summary of Events and Information	Remarks and references to Appendices
1915.		
ROQUETOIRE. Thursday. 23rd Sept:	The spell of fine weather broke in the afternoon when it came on to rain and rained heavily at night.	
	Exchanged G.S. wagon for G.S. limbered wagon for more mobile Transport.	
	2nd Lt. G.S. COURTNEY. R.E. rejoined the Sqdn: on return from sick leave.	
ROQUETOIRE. / MONCHY CAYEUX. Friday. 24th Sept:	The mounted and cyclist portion of the Sqdn: marched at 11.15. a.m. via BLESSY – CUHEM – FEBVIN PALFART to MONCHY CAYEUX. where Advanced 2nd Cav. Div. Report Centre was established at 6. p.m. and connected by cable to Cav. Corps. with S.C. Set. Separate, trivialer superimposed working on a pair of cables. Teed in with Transformer at TANGRY on to ZCO – ST. POL trunk pair. The remainder of the Sqdn: (less an office of 4 men left at ROQUETOIRE as "VB" office with B. Echelon) marched at 3. p.m. to MONCHY – CAYEUX.	
	The Divn: marched after dark to new area South. ("C" area) 3 CB. at HERNICOURT. 4. CB. at BOYAVAL. 5. CB EPS; Divl. Trps. at MONCHY CAYEUX and FLEURY.	
	1. R.F.C. operator and 2 short wave tuners joined for work with aeroplanes. Received 50 coloured rockets for night signals.	[signature] Capt.

(9 29 6) W 2794 100,000 8/14 H W V Forms/C. 2118/11.

Instructions regarding War Diaries and Intelligence Summaries are contained in F. S. Regs., Part II. and the Staff Manual respectively. Title pages will be prepared in manuscript.

WAR DIARY
or
~~INTELLIGENCE SUMMARY.~~
(Erase heading not required.)

2nd SIGNAL SQUADRON * No. .... Date .... * 2nd CAVALRY DIVISION

Army Form C. 2118.

Hour, Date, Place	Summary of Events and Information	Remarks and references to Appendices
1915.		
MONCHY-CATEUX. Friday 25 Sept.	A very wet day all day. In forenoon practised firing of rockets as night signals. Found best and simplest way of firing them to put up telegraph ladder at a slant and laying rocket along it resting on top rung.	
	Conference at Div: HQ. and scheme for offensive given out.	
	At 1.30pm orders were received for the Division to move up and halt in the BOIS DES DAMES. The Division moved in 2 columns. ~~the right~~ via OURTON – BRUAY and the left by PERNES. Owing to blocking of roads by 1st C.D. crossing our front and Guards Div: marching up. the Div: halted and bivouacked	
LOZINGHEM.	3. CB. about MARLES-LEZ-MINES. 4. CB. LA PUGNOY. 5. CB. about CAUCHY-A-LA-TOUR. Div: Troops at LOZINGHEM.	
	Div: Report Centre established at LOZINGHEM at 4. pm. and at 6 pm. connected to Cav: Corps Report Centre (ZRC. at LABUISSIERE) by cable. Other communications by m/cyclist d-r.	
		[illegible] Capt.

(9 29 6) W 2791 100,000 8/14 H W V Forms/C. 2118/11.

Instructions regarding War Diaries and Intelligence Summaries are contained in F. S. Regs., Part II. and the Staff Manual respectively. Title pages will be prepared in manuscript.

WAR DIARY
or
~~INTELLIGENCE SUMMARY.~~
(Erase heading not required.)

2nd SIGNAL SQUADRON No. Date. 2nd CAVALRY DIVISION

Army Form C. 2118.

Hour, Date, Place	Summary of Events and Information	Remarks and references to Appendices
1915.		
LOZINGHEM. Sunday. 26' Sept.	Division are in readiness to move at ½ hours notice. Nothing occurred during the day as regards our division. The ZRC cable was improved and made good during the forenoon. Signal office reliefs take place every 4 hours day and night during operations. It is found that the best results are obtained with this method.	
	The roads were very greasy and bad after the severe rain and heavy traffic. It rained a great deal during the day.	
Monday. 27' Sept.	At 2 am. orders were received for 2. C.D. to be ready to move at 5. am. and 1. C.D. at 6. am. This owing to one of the French Corps about SOUCHEZ having reported ~~r~~ rapid progress. The orders for the move were however cancelled at 4.30. am.	
MARLES-LEZ-MINES.	At 4. pm. our report centre moved to the Mairie. Manager's [illegible] at MARLES-LEZ-MINES; and cable line adjusted accordingly.	
1	It rained steadily all night. At 11.30. pm. orders were recd to be ready to move at 5.30 am. 1. C.D. at 6 am.	SHB Capt.

(9 29 6) W 2794 100,000 8/14 H W V Forms/C. 2118/11.

Instructions regarding War Diaries and Intelligence Summaries are contained in F. S. Regs., Part II. and the Staff Manual respectively. Title pages will be prepared in manuscript.

WAR DIARY
or
~~INTELLIGENCE~~ SUMMARY.
(Erase heading not required.)

Army Form C. 2118.

Hour, Date, Place	Summary of Events and Information	Remarks and references to Appendices
1915.		
MARLES-LEZ-MINES, Tues: Sept. 28th.	The order to be ready to move was cancelled after midnight.	
	The weather was a little better until 5 p.m. when it came on to	
	rain again and poured all night.	
	The division did not move and nothing occurred during the day.	
Wed: Sept. 29th.	A little sun early but it again settled down to rain all day.	
	We received orders to move into a new area about FERFAY and	
	to be clear of our present area (which I.C.D. occupied) by noon.	
	Our report centre established at FERFAY at noon, & then	
FERFAY.	moved to X rds. just N. of M. of WESTREHEM, and at 5 p.m.	
ECQUEDECQUES.	to ECQUEDECQUES. Here Div: HQ. was established.	
	3. CB. at AMETTES 4. CB. at AMES. 5. CB. NEDON. Div. Troops	
	at FERFAY. Cav Corps Adv: Report Centre (R.C.C.) established	
	at ALLOUAGNE at 5. p.m. and connected to us by cable at 8. p.m.	
Thurs: Sept. 30th.	Nothing occurred during the day. Made good cable line – cleaning	
	and drying equipment etc – 16 aeroplanes of ?VOISIN type passed	
	over 2. p.m. going ESE at about 7500 ft. Fine day.	[signature] Capt. 30/9/15.

(9 29 6) W 2791 100,000 8/14 H W V Forms/C. 2118/11.

2nd Cavalry Division

121/7378

G

2nd Signal Squadron R.E.

Vol III

Oct 15

Instructions regarding War Diaries and Intelligence Summaries are contained in F. S. Regs., Part II. and the Staff Manual respectively. Title pages will be prepared in manuscript.

WAR DIARY

~~or~~

~~INTELLIGENCE SUMMARY.~~

~~(Erase heading not required.)~~

2nd SIGNAL SQUADRON
No. ....
Date ....
2nd CAVALRY DIVISION

Army Form C. 2118.

Hour, Date, Place	Summary of Events and Information	Remarks and references to Appendices
1915.		
ECQUEDECQUES. Friday Oct. 1st.	Erected R.F.C. Receiving Station but intercepted no messages.	
Sat. Oct. 2nd.	7.30 am. Large Sqdn. of French aeroplanes of VOISIN type passed over at about 7500 feet going E.S.E. The Division was ordered to send 1000 men to VERMELLES area to clear up the battlefield. This party proceeded by motor bus under command of Bgdr. Gen. F. WORMALD CB. Sent small office under Lr. Peploe for communications of this party, working back to us by telephone through ZRC; "RVB" office being established in NOYELLES-LEZ-VERMELLES.	
ECQUEDECQUES. Sunday. Oct. 3rd. HAM-EN-ARTOIS.	Orders were received for us to vacate ECQUEDECQUES - FERFAY. + AMES to make room for 3. C.D. This was done by 3. pm. Divl: HQ moving to HAM-EN-ARTOIS. and 4. CB. to AUCHY-AU-BOIS. VBR office in ECQUEDECQUES was handed over to YC. and the line to LILLERS was extended to our new office by ZRC. Communication to Brigades all by M/C. d/r. it not being worth while to lay cable lines ~~[illegible]~~ owing to uncertainty of movements; and dispositions of the Brigades. Divl. Troops moved from FERFAY to NORRENT-FONTES. Bgdr. Gen F. WORMALD. CB. killed at VERMELLES.	S.B. Capt.

Instructions regarding War Diaries and Intelligence Summaries are contained in F. S. Regs., Part II. and the Staff Manual respectively. Title pages will be prepared in manuscript.

WAR DIARY
~~or~~
~~INTELLIGENCE SUMMARY.~~
(~~Erase heading not required.~~)

2nd SIGNAL SQUADRON ★ No. .... Date .... 2nd CAVALRY DIVISION

Army Form C. 2118.

Hour, Date, Place	Summary of Events and Information	Remarks and references to Appendices
1915.		
HAM-EN-ARTOIS. Monday. Oct 4th.	Made good cable line to ZRC. building our section to LILLERS.	
	Cpl. JOHNSTONE appointed to temp. Commission in R.E. and gazetted to	
	178th Tunnelling Coy. and left to take up his appointment.	
	Visited VB office. went round units. drew Myogle Stores. Digging parties	rejoined.
Tuesday. Oct. 5th.	Very wet day. Funeral of Bgdr. Gen. F. WORMALD. CB. at NEDONCHELLE. 11 am.	
Wednesday. Oct. 6th.	Usual Routine.	
Thursday. Oct. 7th.	Returned R.F.C. operators and short wave tuners to ZRC for further instruction.	
Friday Oct. 8th. }		
Saturday Oct. 9th. }	Usual Routine. Overhauling Stores etc.	
Sunday. Oct. 10th. }		
Monday. Oct. 11th.	Signallers instruction in instruments etc.	
Tuesday. Oct. 12 }		
Wednesday Oct. 13 }	Usual Routine. Signallers instruction in instruments.	
Thursday. Oct. 14th. }		
Friday Oct. 15th.	Reeled up 2 miles of derelict D.1. cable on AUCHY-AU-BOIS – St HILAIRE road.	
Saturday. Oct. 16th.	Using lorry borrowed from Amm: Park proceeded at 7.30. am. via WALLON CAPPEL	S.W.B. Capt.

(9 29 6) W 2791 100,000 8/14 H W V Forms/C. 2118/11.

Instructions regarding War Diaries and Intelligence Summaries are contained in F. S. Regs., Part II. and the Staff Manual respectively. Title pages will be prepared in manuscript.

WAR DIARY
or
~~INTELLIGENCE SUMMARY.~~
(~~Erase heading not required.~~)

2nd SIGNAL SQUADRON * No. .... Date .... 2nd CAVALRY DIVISION *

Army Form C. 2118.

Hour, Date, Place	Summary of Events and Information	Remarks and references to Appendices
1915.		
HAM-EN-ARTOIS. Saturday Oct. 16th (contd)	with a party of 8 men to NOORDPEENE and reeled up G.I. airline from that place to LE NIEPPE. This was done in 2 hrs. 20 mins. (6 miles) Proceeded to ROQUETOIRE and left stores at VB office.	
ROQUETOIRE. Sunday. Oct. 17th.	Owing to 1st Army requiring HAM-EN-ARTOIS for billeting their own troops Divl: HQ. moved back to ROQUETOIRE. For the same reasons Divl: Troops moved back to ROQUETOIRE area and 4.CB. moved to St ANDRE FM. HAMETZ. BLESSY. etc...	
	The Sqdn: marched at 8.30. am. from HAM-EN-ARTOIS to ROQUETOIRE. VBR closed HAM 10. am. and VB took over at ROQUETOIRE same hour. Reconnoitred 2 routes for airline in proposed billeting area, from ESTREE BLANCHE to St ANDRE FM.	
	In the afternoon the whole Sqdn: was at work overhauling G.I. wire and soldering joints, reeling up local lines, sharpening poles. etc...	
Monday. Oct. 18th.	6. am. Party tarring butts of poles to protect them from damp.	
	7. am. Lt. Sephe with 12 men proceeded by lorry (lent from Amm: Park for 4 days) and laid G.I. airline from St ANDREE FM. via	SWB Capt.

(9 29 6) W 2794 100,000 8/14 H W V Forms/C. 2118/11.

Instructions regarding War Diaries and Intelligence Summaries are contained in F. S. Regs., Part II. and the Staff Manual respectively. Title pages will be prepared in manuscript.

WAR DIARY
~~or~~
~~INTELLIGENCE SUMMARY.~~
(~~Erase heading not required.~~)

Army Form C. 2118.

2nd SIGNAL SQUADRON * No.......... Date.......... 2nd CAVALRY DIVISION *

Hour, Date, Place		Summary of Events and Information	Remarks and references to Appendices
	1915		
ROQUETOIRE.	Monday. Oct. 18th. (contd)	BLESSY. to the main THEROUANNE – ESTREE BLANCHE road. where the line was joined to a disused permanent line at a point ¼' NE of Y in SERNY. The work was finished before dark.	
		Reconnoitred route for line from THIEMBRONNE to DOHEM and selected the northern route via DRIONVILLE and OUVE WIRQUIN where much use can be made of trees at the roadside.	
		Remdr. of Sqdn. in billets reeling up local lines etc —	
	Tuesday Oct. 19th.	Lt. Courtney with 10 men proceeded with lorry 7.15 am. to build G.1. airline from DOHEM via OUVE WIRQUIN & DRIONVILLE to THIEMBRONNE.	
		This line was built as far as LE GRAND MANILLET by dark.	
		Lt. Sepeloe with both wagons proceeded 7.15. am and reeled up cable airline ROQUETOIRE – St ANDRÉ FM. finishing this by 11. am.	
		Divl. Troops marched today to new billets about MERCK. etc –	
		9th Cav. Bde HQ arrived at ROQUETOIRE.	
THIEMBRONNE.	Wednesday Oct. 20th.	7.30. am. Lt. Courtney proceeded with lorry to complete DOHEM – THIEMBRONNE section of line – the whole being then put through and communication opened 5.30. pm.	E.D. Capt.

Instructions regarding War Diaries and Intelligence Summaries are contained in F. S. Regs., Part II. and the Staff Manual respectively. Title pages will be prepared in manuscript.

WAR DIARY
or
~~INTELLIGENCE SUMMARY.~~
(~~Erase heading not required.~~)

2nd SIGNAL SQUADRON No. Date. 2nd CAVALRY DIVISION

Army Form C. 2118.

Hour, Date, Place	Summary of Events and Information	Remarks and references to Appendices
1915.		
THIEMBRONNE. Wednesday Oct. 20. (contd).	Remdr. of Sqdn. marched via CLARQUES - CLETY - AVROULT to new billets, the Sqdn. being billeted at LE BOURGET just SW of THIEMBRONNE. VB closed ROQUETOIRE 10 a.m. and reopened T'BRONNE same hour. Built D.3. cable line to G.S. at HERVARRE CHATEAU. Bdes. marched to new areas. HQ. being:— 3. CB. SANDRE FM. 4. CB. UPEN D'AVAL. 5. CB. PARENTY. a very extended area. and extremely difficult for communications owing to the very long distances for lines and despatch-riders. Line maintenance cannot but be very heavy on the extremely limited personnel provided by establishment for the purpose.	
Thursday Oct. 21.	Stored away stores. Reconnoitred country for lines. Purchased locally some large poles for 3 line trunk down the valley. Issued table of D/R. Services. 2 posts daily to all units. a scheduled time table being prepared.	
Friday. Oct. 22.	Purchased and cut 250 poles from a copse just W. of DRIONVILLE. Party clearing and preparing to build valley trunk line.	SWB. Capt.

(9 29 6) W 2794 100,000 8/14 H W V Forms/C. 2118/11.

Instructions regarding War Diaries and Intelligence Summaries are contained in F. S. Regs., Part II. and the Staff Manual respectively. Title pages will be prepared in manuscript.

WAR DIARY

~~or~~

~~INTELLIGENCE SUMMARY.~~

~~(Erase heading not required.)~~

Army Form C. 2118.

2nd SIGNAL SQUADRON
No. ....
Date ....
2nd CAVALRY DIVISION

Hour, Date, Place	Summary of Events and Information	Remarks and references to Appendices
1915.		
THIEMBRONNE. Saturday. Oct. 23rd.	Overhauled D.5. cable recently picked up. Soldering all joints.	
	Trimmed poles cut yesterday and tarred butts, to protect against wet.	
	Erected and stayed poles for Valley Trunk line. Drew Stores from Cav: Corps.	
Sunday. Oct. 24th.	Fine till 1.pm. but the rest of the day was very wet. Party commenced building pair of G.1. to Gen.Staff at HERVARRE CHÂU. but the work had to be abandoned owing to bad weather.	
	Made 20-line test-board. Got ready terminating pole.	
Monday. Oct. 25th.	Very bad day. Blowing hard and raining. Another 3/4 mile was built of valley line. The gale brought down many lines including ours to ZCO. PC – PD line held till 6.pm. when it was dis: by being broken near CLETY in 2 places.	
Tuesday Oct. 26th.	Reconnoitred route for line to 5th CB. and selected CAMPAGNE – BOURTHES – HUCQUELIERS – ENQUIN. Arranged for line system lines HUCQUELIERS – MONT CAVREL; and HUCQ: – ENQUIN to be used by 5. CB. for communications to regiments. and HUCQ: – BOURTHES pair to be taken over for VB-FE vibrator line.	S.W.B. Capt.

(9 29 6) W 2794 100,000 8/14 H W V Forms/C. 2118/11.

Instructions regarding War Diaries and Intelligence Summaries are contained in F. S. Regs., Part II. and the Staff Manual respectively. Title pages will be prepared in manuscript.

WAR DIARY
or
~~INTELLIGENCE SUMMARY.~~
(Erase heading not required.)

Army Form C. 2118.

Hour, Date, Place	Summary of Events and Information	Remarks and references to Appendices
1915		
THIEMBRONNE. Tuesday. Oct. 26. (contd).	Work on the valley line continued though slow progress only could be made owing to numerous turns, thick hedgerows etc.. However it is considered advisable to hold all lines along the roads so as to facilitate maintenance in the winter.	
Wednesday. Oct. 27.	One party carried on with valley line. Another party of 9 proceeded by lorry to HUCQUELIERS. Whence a cable airline (D.5) was built to S.W.B. at PARENTY. Laying was begun at 8.40 am and the line was finished at 6.20 pm. (7 miles) with ¾ halt for dinner. It is found that ~~the~~ ~~is~~ ¾ mile per hour is about the quickest rate for building cable if it is to be up for some time and is tied in at each tree etc... with equipment in possession of a Signal Sqdn.	
	2 linemen overhauled the HUCQUELIERS - BOURTHES permanent line, which was in a bad state and quite un-maintained. broken insulators. etc... and a great deal of tree clearing had to be done. This permanent line (one leg) was put through onto cable line and proved at the end of the day.	S.W.B. Capt.

Instructions regarding War Diaries and Intelligence Summaries are contained in F. S. Regs., Part II. and the Staff Manual respectively. Title pages will be prepared in manuscript.

WAR DIARY
or
~~INTELLIGENCE SUMMARY.~~

(~~Erase heading not required.~~)

Army Form C. 2118.

2nd SIGNAL SQUADRON
No.
Date
2nd CAVALRY DIVISION

Hour, Date, Place	Summary of Events and Information	Remarks and references to Appendices
1915.		
THIEMBRONNE. Thursday. Oct. 28th.	A very wet day all day and blowing hard. In spite of the weather cable party started out with lorry at 8:30 am and built D.S. airline to CAMPAGNE and on to BOURTHES where it was put through on to the permanent line. and communication established with PE at 6. pm. 12th Lancers at CAMPAGNE Teed in intermediate.	
	Pair of G.I. wires to HERVARRE were completed during the day by another party. PC-PD line dis near CLETY after dark.	
Friday. Oct. 29th.	Rigged and placed terminating derrick opposite Signal office. Completed internal wiring of Signal office.	
Saturday. Oct. 30th.	Built new section of PC-PD line G.I. to half way to DRIONVILLE reeling up the cable which had been temporarily used for last mile. 10. am changed over all instruments to new connections and everything correct and Signals O.K.	
	Put through metallic circuit pair to G.S. Built lines to local offices.	Cut 150 poles in forest.
Sunday. Oct. 31st.	Completed local office lines and tested instruments.	

[signature] Capt.
Cmdg: Signals. 2nd Cav. Div.

(6114) Wt. W3906/P1607 2,500,000 7/18 McA & W Ltd (E 3591) Forms W3091/4. Army Form W.3091.

Cover for Documents.

265

Nature of Enclosures.

War Diary

of

2nd. Sig Sqdn. R.E.

Period :- Nov. 1915.

Notes, or Letters written.

Instructions regarding War Diaries and Intelligence Summaries are contained in F. S. Regs., Part II. and the Staff Manual respectively. Title pages will be prepared in manuscript.

WAR DIARY

or

~~INTELLIGENCE SUMMARY.~~

~~(Erase heading not required.)~~

Army Form C. 2118.

286

Hour, Date, Place	Summary of Events and Information	Remarks and references to Appendices
1915		
THIENBRONNE. Monday Nov. 1st.	Very wet day and blowing hard. One party [illegible] from [illegible] [illegible] to St MARTIN. (Left [illegible] during the day.) Another party of 3 "[illegible]" accompanied Signal Co. to LE NIEPPE and [illegible] a pair of D1 cable to the Artillery. Then [illegible] up 3 [illegible] [illegible] to RENESCURE and [illegible] [illegible] [illegible] HAZEBROUCK, St OMER, LUMBRES and exchange. [illegible] communication with VB [illegible] obtained, the average time for getting through being 4 minutes.	
	Issued new Schedule of D.R. Service on new system. The new system which has proved very successful is worked as follows. On arrival in a new billeting area the [illegible] is carefully studied so as to discover how units can conveniently be visited by one D.R. on the same journey with due regard to the no. of times per diem the various units [illegible] to be visited, and at what hours. This being decided, a good [illegible] is drawn up to [illegible] the time and "[illegible]" carefully going very slow. ¼ hour is then added to each of the times between places so as to allow for [illegible] [illegible] and [illegible] at units.	[illegible initials]

Instructions regarding War Diaries and Intelligence Summaries are contained in F. S. Regs., Part II. and the Staff Manual respectively. Title pages will be prepared in manuscript.

WAR DIARY

or

~~INTELLIGENCE SUMMARY.~~

~~(Erase heading not required.)~~

2nd SIGNAL SQUADRON · No. ____ Date ____ · 2nd CAVALRY DIVISION

Army Form C. 2118.

287

Hour, Date, Place	Summary of Events and Information	Remarks and references to Appendices
1915		
THIEMBRONNE. Mon. Nov. 1st (contd).	The time of departure from each unit in the [illegible] area and a schedule prepared accordingly and issued to all concerned. † It is found that with this system the D.R. services can be very punctual to schedule, an error of more than 5 minutes being rare. It is also found very economical in petrol and mechanical wear of m/cycles.	† Copy of schedule for [illegible] [illegible] end of month attached. Appendix I
Tuesday Nov. 2nd.	A very wet day all day, and wiring on the line out of the question. Drew stores from Cav. Corps Signals.	
Wednesday Nov. 3rd.	Completed [illegible] wire [illegible] to A.S.C. offices at St MARTIN. Reorganized the Squadron into 4 sections, each under a Corporal. This for purposes of signal office duty and line maintenance. Thus the duties on the first day are as follows:—	
	A. Section provide H.Q. N.C.O. (supplies) operators, orderly & W/T, duty linemen and W/T [illegible] & patrols local lines.	
	B. Section provide W/T N.C.O. (supplies) & emergency linemen, patrols [illegible] Hesdin line & PE line.	
	C. Section patrols ZCO line, PC–PD line.	
	D. Section, Reserve, provides working party if required.	
		[illegible]

(9 29 6) W 2794 100,000 8/14 H W V Forms/C. 2118/11.

Instructions regarding War Diaries and Intelligence Summaries are contained in F. S. Regs., Part II. and the Staff Manual respectively. Title pages will be prepared in manuscript.

WAR DIARY
or
~~INTELLIGENCE SUMMARY.~~
~~(Erase heading not required.)~~

2nd SIGNAL SQUADRON
No. ____
Date ____
2nd CAVALRY DIVISION

Army Form C. 2118.

288

Hour, Date, Place		Summary of Events and Information	Remarks and references to Appendices
	1915		
THIEMBRONNE.	Thursday Nov. 4th.	Dull day and a good deal of rain. Made good Valley [illegible] line, and put guards on at all angles.	
	Friday Nov. 5.	Usual Routine.	
	Saturday Nov. 6.	Strengthening lines etc.	
	Sunday Nov. 7.	B Section marched to S. ANDRE FM. (H.Q. 3 CB) and built D.S. cable line to Supply Column at S. QUENTIN as an extension of present circuit. B Section billeted at S. ANDRE FM.	
	Monday Nov. 8.	B Section at work all day from S. ANDRE FM. to DUVE W.ROUIN. Digging in old poles, staying every other pole, and generally strengthening the line.	
	Tuesday Nov. 9.	C Section completed their work to VB. by 4 pm. Showery dull day.	
	Wednesday Nov. 10.	Usual Routine.	
	Thursday Nov. 11.	Cable line to PE at PARENTY carefully inspected but no strengthening required.	
	Friday Nov. 12.	All lines complete and strengthened against any weather, for the winter. Received information that Divisional Billeting area is to be entirely changed. Very wet day and blowing hard.	[initials]

Instructions regarding War Diaries and Intelligence Summaries are contained in F. S. Regs., Part II. and the Staff Manual respectively. Title pages will be prepared in manuscript.

WAR DIARY
or
INTELLIGENCE SUMMARY.
(Erase heading not required.)

Army Form C. 2118.

289

Hour, Date, Place	Summary of Events and Information	Remarks and references to Appendices
1915.		
THIEMBRONNE Saturday. Nov. 13.	Lt PEPLOE left the Sqdn. to assume command of 9th Signal Troop. Still blowing hard. Wiring parties out all day adjusting damages by gale.	
Sunday. Nov. 14.	After a sharp frost a very cold day. Lt COURTNEY with B Section built cross-line air line from ½ mile S of DRIONVILLE on present line (PC-PD) to NIELLES-LEZ-BLEQUIN, which is to be new HQ of 4 C.B. This was finished all except the last 1200x before dark. Progress being rather slow owing to digging all poles in about 3 ft. & staying every second pole. The new section are being built of iron-wire. It being found that the Galvanized iron wire has the following disadvantages.	
	(1) It stretches very considerably with strain on.	
	(2). Very liable to break with swinging of Fire etc...	
	(3). Kinks badly in laying; and, once kinked, breaks immediately.	
	(4). Will not stand much straining.	
Monday. Nov. 15.	B Section left by lorry (lent from Ammn. Park) at 4 pm. Lt PARROTT ready to reel up D.S. cable air line on 5 Pole morning tomorrow. A Section completed airline to NIELLES-LEZ-BLEQUIN. Very cold day.	SHB

(9 29 6) W 2794 100,000 8/14 H W V Forms/C. 2118/11.

Instructions regarding War Diaries and Intelligence Summaries are contained in F. S. Regs., Part II. and the Staff Manual respectively. Title pages will be prepared in manuscript.

WAR DIARY
or
~~INTELLIGENCE SUMMARY.~~
(Erase heading not required.)

2nd SIGNAL SQUADRON · No. ____ Date ____ · 2nd CAVALRY DIVISION

Army Form C. 2118.

290

Hour, Date, Place	Summary of Events and Information	Remarks and references to Appendices
THIEMBRONNE 1915 Tuesday Nov. 16.	Between 11.30 pm last night and 6.30 am today 7 inches of snow had fallen. It speaks much for [illegible] communication that [illegible] were at work on the roads by 8 am. [illegible] could not move. So the D.R. service was executed by the 2nd Dragoon Guards and ran punctually.	
	The 1 Cav. Div. moved to their new billeting area (HQ at SAMER) and 5 Cav. Bde moved to the new area. HQ at FAUQUEMBERGUES. The roads were in a very bad state for marching. There was practically no snow at all, east of THEROUANNE.	
	B. Section, though delayed in starting owing to lorry being unable to move through the snow, picked up the section of line from PARENTY to HUCQUELIERS by 3 pm. when they were sent home, but the lorry [illegible] near RUMILLY and [illegible] the night there.	
	[illegible] and handed back to French Civil authorities.	
	Communication with 5 CB. temporarily by extension of A.S.C. line.	
	Captain P H KERANS handed command of 4 Signal Troop on appointment as Staff Captain 7 Cav. Bde. and was temporarily replaced by Lt. J HALLIDAY 11 Hussars.	
	Issued new schedule of D.R. service for new area.	(Appendix I.) [illegible]

(9 29 6)* W 2794 100,000 8/14 H W V Forms/C. 2118/11.

Instructions regarding War Diaries and Intelligence Summaries are contained in F. S. Regs., Part II. and the Staff Manual respectively. Title pages will be prepared in manuscript.

WAR DIARY

or

~~INTELLIGENCE SUMMARY.~~

(~~Erase heading not required.~~)

Army Form C. 2118.

2ND SIGNAL SQUADRON
No. ....
Date ....
2ND CAVALRY DIVISION

291

Hour, Date, Place	Summary of Events and Information	Remarks and references to Appendices
1915	Thawing.	
THIEMBRONNE. Wednesday Nov 17.	3 Cos moved from St ANDRE FM to OUVE WIRQUIN. 4 Cos from UPEN D'AVAL to [illegible] LEZ BLEQUIN. Supply Coln. from S. QUENTIN to ESQUERDES.	
	Amm Park to AVROULT. Railhead from AIRE to WIZERNES.	
	C Section proceeded at 8 am to RUMILLY. Got [illegible] from lorry and constructed	
	DS cable air line from X roads on the T'BRONNE – CAMPAGNE road (then being TL on the VB – TL line — TL being [illegible] at CAMPAGNE) to PE at FAUQUEMBERGUES.	
	This work was finished at 4 pm.	
	Small [illegible] parties with lorry [illegible] in the forenoon put supply column at	
	ESQUERDES on to 2ND Exchange by extending an existing [illegible] with 2 DS line	
	through the village.	
	Lorry was got out by Supply Column breakdown lorry during the forenoon, and	
	left at 4 pm with D Section for S ANDRE FM. [illegible] the night.	
Thursday. Nov 18.	After breakfast in [illegible] till 3 pm [illegible]	
	D Section began work at S ANDRE 7.15 am and reeled up DS line to St QUENTIN	
	and then reeled up G1 [illegible] THÉROUANNE [illegible] by 1.30 pm. [illegible]	
	proceeded to DOHEM and reeled up G1 [illegible] to OUVE WIRQUIN finishing 4.55 pm.	[initials]

Instructions regarding War Diaries and Intelligence Summaries are contained in F. S. Regs., Part II. and the Staff Manual respectively. Title pages will be prepared in manuscript.

WAR DIARY

or

~~INTELLIGENCE SUMMARY.~~

~~(Erase heading not required.)~~

2nd SIGNAL SQUADRON No. ...... Date ...... 2nd CAVALRY DIVISION

Army Form C. 2118.

292

Hour, Date, Place	Summary of Events and Information	Remarks and references to Appendices
1915		
THIEMBRONNE. Friday November 19.	After a hard frost it was a fine day but overcast. Usual Routine.	
Saturday Nov. 20.	Orders received for organization of a dismounted division from Cav Corps.	
Sunday Nov. 21.	Completed organization of signal arrangements for Bde to be furnished for dismounted div.	
Monday Nov. 22.	Completed tree clearing on new air line. Fine day after a hard frost.	
Tuesday Nov. 23.	Overhauled all D.5. cable and D3 cable. Fine day. Rained at night.	
Wednesday Nov. 24.	Overhauled all wire and reeled off from cable on to drums. It being easier to lay from drums as it runs better.	
Thursday Nov 25.	Completed overhaul of wire line. Fitted leather washers to all nails for bobbin insulators in trees. Found that by doing so not only is the bobbin tightly held and prevented from turning round, but also the leakage of bobbins when nailing them to trees is reduced to a minimum.	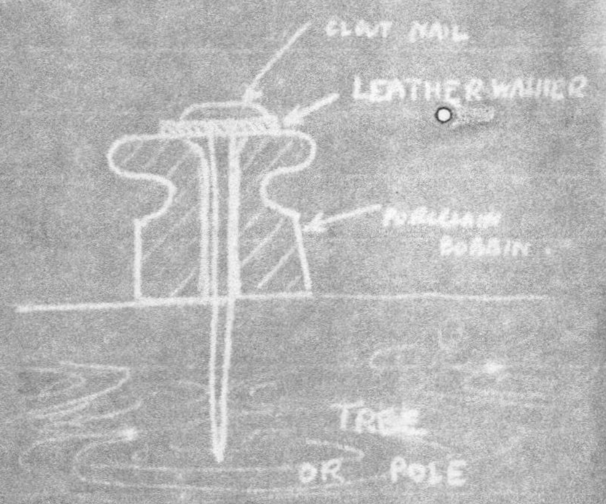
Friday Nov. 26.	Usual Routine. 2 snow storms.	
Saturday Nov. 27.	Usual Routine. Hard frost.	
Sunday Nov. 28.	Usual Routine.	
Monday Nov. 29.	Party overhauling telegraph line and rebuilt at station. Rained all day.	
Tuesday Nov 30.	Squadron attended demonstration of effectiveness of [illegible] tube helmets against gas at FAUQUEMBERGUES.	[illegible] Capt. 30/11/15 Comdg Signal Sqdn 2 Cav Div.

(9 29 6) W 2794 100,000 8/14 H W V Forms/C. 2118/11.

2nd Signal Sqn. (2nd Cav. Dn)

Dec 1915

Vol. V

Instructions regarding War Diaries and Intelligence Summaries are contained in F. S. Regs., Part II. and the Staff Manual respectively. Title pages will be prepared in manuscript.

WAR DIARY
~~or~~
~~INTELLIGENCE SUMMARY.~~
(*Erase ~~heading not required.~~*)

Army Form C. 2118.

2nd SIGNAL SQUADRON
No. ....
Date. ....
2nd CAVALRY DIVISION

Hour, Date, Place		Summary of Events and Information	Remarks and references to Appendices
	1915.		
THIEMBRONNE.	Wed. Decr 1st.	"D" Section strengthening Valley Trunk line. A very windy day.	
	Thurs. Decr 2nd.	Usual Routine. Sapper Cooper to ZCO for Course of Wireless Telegraphy.	
	Friday. Decr 3rd.	Very wet day and blowing hard. Usual Routine.	
	Sat. Decr 4th.	ditto.	
	Sun. Decr 5th.	Working parties on PD & valley trunk line, which had suffered from the gale.	
	Mon. Decr 6.	Working party on PC line. (B Secn.) A Secn. on G.S. line.	
	Tues. Decr 7.	Continued wet weather. Usual Routine.	
	Wed. Decr 8.	Fine day. Usual Routine.	
	Thurs. Decr 9.	Very wet all day. Party made good cable line to PE.	
	Friday. Decr 10.	Again wet all day. Party cutting gorse for improving stables.	
	Sat. Decr 11.	Wet all day. Party repairing stabling with gorse hurdle work.	
	Sun. Decr 12.	Usual Routine. Church Parade Service MERCK. 2.30. pm.	
	Mon. Decr 13.	After a frost fine day. B Secn. repairing stable floors with rubble etc. Worked out equipment to be carried by "dismounted" Signal Troop.	
	Tues. Decr 14.	At home conference of Signal officers of the division to discuss equipment for dismounted Signal Troop. Fine.	

Instructions regarding War Diaries and Intelligence Summaries are contained in F. S. Regs., Part II. and the Staff Manual respectively. Title pages will be prepared in manuscript.

WAR DIARY

~~or~~

~~INTELLIGENCE SUMMARY.~~

(~~Erase heading not required.~~)

Army Form C. 2118.

Hour, Date, Place	Summary of Events and Information	Remarks and references to Appendices
1915		
THIEMBRONNE. Wed. Decr. 15th.	Very cold day & some sleet. Conference of Brigadiers at OUVE WIRQUIN 11.30 am. at which the question of providing Signal Officers was discussed. "D" Section cutting gorse for stable improvements.	
Thurs. Decr. 16th.	Usual Routine. Foggy day.	
Friday. Decr. 17th.	O.C. visited R.H.A. batteries about LOCON. etc.. and distributed telephone stores. Squadron had baths, & clothing disinfected. Wet day.	
Sat. Decr. 18th.	Fine but foggy. At 9-30 am the dismounted Signal Troop rendezvoused at CLOQUANT under Lt. Halliday, and was inspected by O.C.	
Sun. Decr. 19th.	Usual Routine. Church Parade at MERCK 5.30 pm.	
Mon. Decr. 20th.	Fine. Usual Routine.	
Tues. Decr. 21st.	All horses innoculated for mallein test. 2nd Lt. F.F. MOORE. 6.D.G. joined for a few days instruction prior to assuming temporary command of 4th Sig. Tp.	
Wed. Decr. 22nd.	Horses inspected at 24 hours after mallein test. No reaction.	
Thurs. Decr. 23rd.	Wet day. A Squadron boxing competition was held - there being 16 entries for 3 weights. The boxing was excellent. G.O.C. attended and gave away the prizes after the finals at 9.30. pm.	

Instructions regarding War Diaries and Intelligence Summaries are contained in F. S. Regs., Part II. and the Staff Manual respectively. Title pages will be prepared in manuscript.

WAR DIARY

~~or~~

~~INTELLIGENCE SUMMARY.~~

(Erase heading not required.)

2nd SIGNAL SQUADRON
No. ....
Date ....
2nd CAVALRY DIVISION

Army Form C. 2118.

Hour, Date, Place	Summary of Events and Information	Remarks and references to Appendices
1915		
THIEMBRONNE. Friday Dec. 24.	2nd Lt. MOORE. 6th D.G. rejoined his regt. Lt. J. HALLIDAY. 11th Hrs. temporarily lent from 3rd Sig. Sqdn. vacates command of 4th Sig. Tp. Usual Routine. and preparations for Christmas.	
Saturday Dec. 25.	CHRISTMAS DAY. Church parade MERCK. 11 am. A showery day. O.C. saw some mens dinners at 1 pm. A smoking concert was held in the School from 6 – 9 pm. in conjunction with the HQ. details. The G.O.C. attended.	
Sunday. Dec. 26.	Fine till 6.30 pm when it rained all night. Sent stores up to batteries of 3rd Bde. R.H.A. and also sent lineman up to overhaul and test all the telephones of the batteries.	
Monday Dec. 27.	Windy and showery day. Orders were received for the Dismounted Division to be concentrated in billets by 6 pm 28th. Digging parties recalled. Prepared table of battalion signalling equipment. assembled Signal officers and issued telephone equipment for battalions. Lt. EVETTS Oxfordshire Hussars joined for 12 days course of instruction prior to attending course at Cav. Corps. Capt. E. Beddington 16. L. replaced Capt. Musgrave as G.S.O.2.	[signature]

(9 29 6) W 2794 100,000 8/14 H W V Forms/C. 2118/11.

Army Form C. 2118.

Instructions regarding War Diaries and Intelligence Summaries are contained in F. S. Regs., Part II. and the Staff Manual respectively. Title pages will be prepared in manuscript.

WAR DIARY
or
INTELLIGENCE SUMMARY.
(*Erase heading not required.*)

Hour, Date, Place	Summary of Events and Information	Remarks and references to Appendices
1915		
THIEMBRONNE. Tuesday. 28th Dec.	Lt. W.M. CODRINGTON. 16th Lancers. assumed Command of 5th Sig. Tp. vice Captain Viscount EBRINGTON. R.S. Greys (appointed S.C. 1st Cav Bde). Pnt Fieldsqdn. or intermediate r.A.S.C. line.	
Wednesday. 29th Dec.	Fine but colder. 5 men sent to ZCO. as part of HQ. & 20.1 Sect. of Composite Signal Sqdn. for Dismounted Divn. at 3. pm. Cpl. CLARKE. RE. joined Sqdn from PE. on promotion.	
Thursday. 30th Dec.	No 3. Section Composite Signal Sqdn. assembled at HQ. 4. CB. (HQ. of 2nd Dismounted Bde.) at 9.30 am under 2/Lt. COURTNEY. It was then inspected by O.C. Signals.	
Friday 31st Dec.	Fine day. HQ. 2nd Dismounted Bde. & 4th Battalion entrained and proceeded for the trenches.	

John Offord Blane [signature]
Captain
Comdg Signals 2nd Cav. Div.
1st January. 1916

2 Cav

2nd Signal Sqn.

Jan 1916.

Vol. VI

Instructions regarding War Diaries and Intelligence Summaries are contained in F. S. Regs., Part II. and the Staff Manual respectively. Title pages will be prepared in manuscript.

WAR DIARY
or
~~INTELLIGENCE~~ SUMMARY.
(*Erase heading not required.*)

Army Form C. 2118.

Hour, Date, Place	Summary of Events and Information	Remarks and references to Appendices
1916.		
THIEMBRONNE. Sat. Jan. 1st	Usual Routine. One lineman sent to 3rd Bde. R.H.A. to inspect and overhaul telephones.	
Sun Jan 2nd	Blowing hard and raining. 3rd + 5th Battalions of 2nd Dismounted Bde. entrained for the trenches.	
Mon. Jan 3rd	Connected A.S.C. to PE exchange pro tem. having decided to reel up valley trunk line owing to frequent breaking of G.L. wire on the trees. "D" Section then commenced to reel up valley trunk line starting from HERVARRE and completed as far as "White House Testing Station" by dark. Very windy day.	
Tuesday. Jan 4th	Completed dismantling and reeling up valley trunk line. Wet day.	
Wed: Jan 5th	Fine day all day. Prepared Stores for new trunk line to be built via CLOQUANT and over the hill to HERVARRE. The new 3-line trunk is carried on rough poles. One line on a bobbin screwed on the top of the pole. The other two one at each end of a 20" yard clamped onto the pole with the spare bolts & clamps obtained from "Semi-permanent" brackets in cases where these brackets have been bolted back to back.	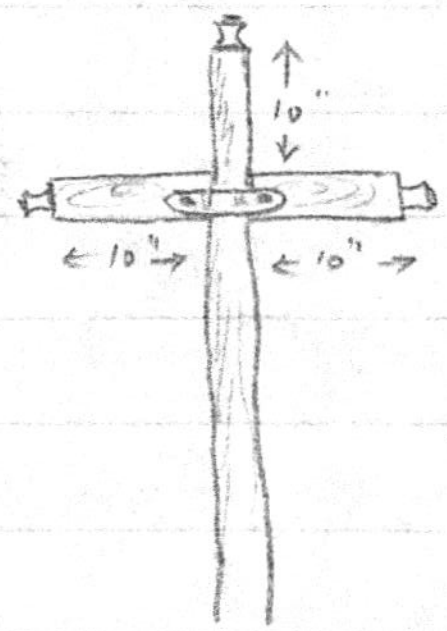

SmB

(9 29 6) W 2794 100,000 8/14 H W V Forms/C. 2118/11.

Instructions regarding War Diaries and Intelligence Summaries are contained in F. S. Regs., Part II. and the Staff Manual respectively. Title pages will be prepared in manuscript.

WAR DIARY
~~or~~
~~INTELLIGENCE SUMMARY.~~
(Erase heading not required.)

Army Form C. 2118.

2nd SIGNAL SQUADRON
No. ....
Date ....
2nd CAVALRY DIVISION

Hour, Date, Place	Summary of Events and Information	Remarks and references to Appendices
1916.		
~~Wednesday.~~ THIEMBRONNE. Wed. Jan. 5th (contd)	The ~~late~~ leather washers suggested in my War Diary under date 25/11/15 have been adopted by Signal Park and are now issued with the bobbins.	
Thursday. Jan 6th.	Blowing hard and raining all day. Adjusted 2CO line clear of village — fitted brackets with black insulators to carry 5 lines on houses etc. — O.C. proceeded to SAILLY LA BOURSE and VERMELLES and inspected communications of 2nd Dismounted Bde.	
Friday Jan 7th.	Windy day. Prepared poles, yards etc. — for new trunk line.	
Saturday Jan 8.	Fine day. Commenced new trunk line, and erected all poles to the CLOQUANT turn and built up line at same time. Then deflected 2CO pair so as to shorten that line & follow same course, the two lines now running parallel to each other and 10 yds apart. Built new line with 100 lb. iron wire — 50 yard bays. Stays being arranged as follows:— 4 stays, 2 wind, 2 line, 2 wind, 4 stays and so on.	
Sunday Jan 9th	Prepared more stores for continuation of line. LT. H. E. EVETTS Oxfordshire Hussars proceeded to 2CO for course — also Lts. STIRLING-STEWART R.S. Greys; SMITH 4th Hussars; RAWNSLEY 12th Lancers and F.F. MOORE 6 DGs (14 Sig Tp).	[illegible] Capt

(9 29 6) W 2794 100,000 8/14 H W V Forms/C. 2118/11.

Instructions regarding War Diaries and Intelligence Summaries are contained in F. S. Regs., Part II. and the Staff Manual respectively. Title pages will be prepared in manuscript.

WAR DIARY

or

~~INTELLIGENCE SUMMARY.~~

(*Erase heading not required.*)

2nd SIGNAL SQUADRON, No. ... Date ... 2nd CAVALRY DIVISION

Army Form C. 2118.

Hour, Date, Place	Summary of Events and Information	Remarks and references to Appendices
1916		
THIEMBRONNE. Mon: Jan 10.	Dull and cold. Continued new trunk line – and erected all poles up to HERVARRE angle – and thence on to HERVARRE CH^TE – and built top line same time.	
Tues: Jan. 11.	Cold and windy. Reeled up old G.S.C. line from WILLAMETZ to HERVARRE – FAUQUEMBERGUES road – and then built a new line from this point to HERVARRE and joined up with top line of new trunk line. Then built G.S. pair as far as HERVARRE angle. Received news of the successful evacuation of the Dardanelles and also of the loss of H.M.S. "King Edward VII."	
Wed. Jan. 12.	After a light frost a fine cold day till 3 pm. then it rained. Built G.S. pair as far as the old rifle range 600^x outside the village.	
Thursday. Jan 13.	V. cold day. and blowing hard. Completed new trunk line. Constructed new buzzer telephone with a strong G.S.C. buzzer and certain D.2. telephone parts – and tested it on Bde. lines. It proved to be superior to the existing "D" telephones though not so strong a buzz as the vibrator	S.H.B.

(9 29 6) W 2794 100,000 8/14 H W V Forms/C. 2118/11.

Instructions regarding War Diaries and Intelligence Summaries are contained in F. S. Regs., Part II. and the Staff Manual respectively. Title pages will be prepared in manuscript.

WAR DIARY

~~or~~

~~INTELLIGENCE SUMMARY.~~

(*Erase heading not required.*)

Army Form C. 2118.

2nd SIGNAL SQUADRON No. Date. 2nd CAVALRY DIVISION

Hour, Date, Place		Summary of Events and Information	Remarks and references to Appendices
	1916		
THIEMBRONNE.	Friday Jan. 14.	Fine day. Usual Routine.	
	Saturday Jan. 15.	Fine. Lt. Courtney relieved by Lt. Codrington (5th Sig. Tp.) as Sig. Offr of 2nd Dism: Bde.	
	Sunday Jan. 16.	Raining and windy. Usual Routine.	
	Monday Jan 17.	Labelled all lines at ends, crossings, and test stations.	
	Tuesday Jan. 18 } Wednesday Jan. 19 }	Marking all stays of new trunk line with brushwood.	
	Thursday Jan. 20 to Monday Jan 31.	Usual Routine. No training possible owing to shortage of men. Most of working men being with dismounted Divn.	

J. Wentworth Blake

Captain.

Cmdg Signals 2nd Cav Divn

31/1/16.

(9 29 6) W 2794 100,000 8/14 H W V Forms/C. 2118/11.

Instructions regarding War Diaries and Intelligence Summaries are contained in F. S. Regs., Part II. and the Staff Manual respectively. Title pages will be prepared in manuscript.

WAR DIARY
~~or~~
~~INTELLIGENCE~~ SUMMARY.
(~~Erase heading not required.~~)

2nd SIGNAL SQUADRON * 2nd CAVALRY DIVISION *

Army Form C. 2118.

Hour, Date, Place	Summary of Events and Information	Remarks and references to Appendices
1916. THIEMBRONNE		
Tuesday. Feb. 1st. / Wed. Feb. 2nd. / Thurs. Feb 3rd.	Usual Routine. Weather very cold but fine.	
Friday. Feb. 4th.	Blowing a S.S.E. gale and raining hard. O.C. went by motor to VERMELLES to arrange for reliefs of men of 2nd Div. Bde. Signal Section and also to see communications.	
Sat. Feb. 5th	Lt. Codrington (5th Sig. Tp.) proceeded to trenches to relieve Lt. Rice (3rd Sig Tp.) as O.C. Signals 2nd Div. Bde.	
Sun. Feb. 6th. / Mon. Feb. 7th. / Tues. Feb. 8th.	Usual Routine	
Wed. Feb. 9th.	O.C. proceeded to 3rd Army for a week's attachment to Signal Units and proceeded to 7th Divn. at TREUX. Usual Routine	
Thurs. Feb. 10th.	Usual Routine. O.C. with 7th Divn. Sig. Coy went round Bde. Comms: Report centres. Signal offices etc... Saw system of burying lines etc... in area MORLANCOURT - BRAY - MEAULTE - GIBRALTAR etc...	

(9 29 6) W 2794 100,000 8/14 H W V Forms/C. 2118/11.

Instructions regarding War Diaries and Intelligence Summaries are contained in F. S. Regs., Part II. and the Staff Manual respectively. Title pages will be prepared in manuscript.

WAR DIARY

~~or~~

~~INTELLIGENCE SUMMARY.~~

(Erase heading not required.)

Army Form C. 2118.

2nd SIGNAL SQUADRON No. .... Date .... 2nd CAVALRY DIVISION

Hour, Date, Place	Summary of Events and Information	Remarks and references to Appendices
1916. THIEMBRONNE.		
Friday. Feb. 11th.	Usual Routine. O.C. with 7th Divn: inspected instruments. improvised exchanges. Artillery offices etc....	
Sat. Feb. 12th.	Usual Routine. O.C. with 7th Divn; discussed communications employed by 7th Divn during Battle of Loos. etc... O.C proceeded in evening to be attached to 30th Divn: at ETINHEM.	
Sunday. Feb. 13th.	Usual Routine. O.C with 30 Divn: inspected local Signal Offices. instruments etc.... and saw lines laid in river SOMME towards SUZANNE etc...	
Monday. Feb. 14th.	Usual Routine. O.C. with 30th Divn: rode round Bdes. and saw Bde and R.A. Signal Offices. report centres etc... at SUZANNE. BRAY-BRONFAY FM. etc... and in the evening proceeded to be attached to 13th Corps at HEILLY.	
Tuesday. Feb. 15.	Dismounted Division returned from the trenches to billets. O.C with 13th Corps inspected lines and signal offices. Saw wireless stations at work. instruments etc...	
Wednesday. Feb. 16.	Usual Routine. O.C. with 13th Corps. went through all details of Sig. office and organization. and returned to VB. seeing 3rd Army Signal Office en route.	GWB.

(9 29 6) W 2794 100,000 8/14 H W V Forms/C. 2118/11.

Instructions regarding War Diaries and Intelligence Summaries are contained in F. S. Regs., Part II. and the Staff Manual respectively. Title pages will be prepared in manuscript.

WAR DIARY

~~or~~

~~INTELLIGENCE SUMMARY.~~

(*Erase heading not required.*)

Army Form C. 2118.

Hour, Date, Place	Summary of Events and Information	Remarks and references to Appendices
1916 THIEMBRONNE.		
Thursday Feb. 17. } Friday Feb. 18. }	Usual Routine.	
Sat. Feb. 19.	Eight regimental officers tested to ascertain their knowledge of "small flag" and "buzzer" with a view to their attending a course of instruction.	
Sun. Feb. 20.	Usual Routine. O.C. visited Bde. Signal Troops.	
Mon. Feb. 21.	Usual Routine. Saddle inspection etc... All Battalion Telephone equipment returned to Cav: Corps. This is very serious as Cavalry regiments cannot possibly be trained in telephone without equipment.	
Tues. Feb. 22.	It had snowed during the night and snowed all day. Arms inspection. Ammn: Park and batteries marched back from BETHUNE area to billets.	
Wed. Feb. 23. } Thurs. Feb. 24. }	Prepared amendments to T.M.S. Prov: 1915. with a view to standardizing and modernizing Signal procedure. and submitted them to Cav: Corps. Signals.	
Friday. Feb. 25.	Hard frost. Wireless unable to run so using Singer Cars for d/r. Wireless inspected by O.C. Supply Colm.	
Sat. Feb. 26.	Many roads impassable through drifts. Constructed and employed single horse sleighs with success. Thaw set in in the afternoon, and it thawed during the night. Snowed all the afternoon & evening	SWB Capt.

Instructions regarding War Diaries and Intelligence Summaries are contained in F. S. Regs., Part II. and the Staff Manual respectively. Title pages will be prepared in manuscript.

WAR DIARY

~~or~~

~~INTELLIGENCE SUMMARY.~~

(~~Erase heading not required.~~)

Army Form C. 2118.

Hour, Date, Place	Summary of Events and Information	Remarks and references to Appendices
THIEMBRONNE.		
1916 Sunday. Feb. 27.	Thawing all day. Church parade 11. a.m. 2/Lt. A.A.T. BRAND 12th Lers joined the Sqdn: from Home Signal Depot. 5 Sigs. joined from Regts.	
Monday. Feb. 28.	Thawed all day and rained a little in the evening. Motorcycles able to run again. O.C. inspected Divisional Lines. Laid line of old D5. cable and connected up Field Sqdn: to Exchange. Rearranged billeting accommodation of Sqdn.	
Tuesday. Feb. 29.	Roads & country practically clear of snow. Bicycle and Arms inspection. Sqdn: parade to give out details of training to commence tomorrow. Received amendments to T.M.S. back from Cav. Corps approved. and issued them to all units.	
	1/3/16.	[illegible] Captain. Cmdg Signals. 2nd Cav Div

(9 29 6) W 2794 100,000 8/14 H W V Forms/C. 2118/11.

Instructions regarding War Diaries and Intelligence Summaries are contained in F. S. Regs., Part II. and the Staff Manual respectively. Title pages will be prepared in manuscript.

WAR DIARY ~~or~~ ~~INTELLIGENCE SUMMARY.~~

(~~Erase heading not required.~~)

Army Form C. 2118.

Hour, Date, Place	Summary of Events and Information	Remarks and references to Appendices
1916		
THIEMBRONNE. Wed: March 1st.	Signal Training in 2nd Cav. Div. began. All signal units, each regt: signallers commencing usual training.	
	Sig: Sqdn. Flag drill. Lecture on new procedure. Buzzer reading. Lamp reading.	
Thurs. March 2nd. Friday. March 3rd.	Flag and shutter reading and flag drill. Lamp reading.	
Sat. March 4th.	Snow and sleet all day. Buzzer reading etc...	
Sun. March 5th.	Usual routine. Cav: Corps having been broken up and 2nd Cav. Div. allotted to 2nd Army. we came under orders of 2nd Army at midnight 5/6. O.C. visited D.D.A.S. 2nd Army at Cassel to arrange matters on coming under his orders.	
Mon: March 6th.	An inch of snow had fallen during the night. Several heavy snowstorms in the forenoon. Thawed during the afternoon and then froze hard all night. Pairs work flag and shutter in forenoon. Helio and large flag reading & lamps p.m.	
	Conference of Bde. Signal Offrs. 11.30. am. to discuss supply of stores, personnel etc.. under new régime and also various other points in connection with training. Equipment etc --	[signature] Capt.

(9 29 6) W 2794 100,000 8/14 H W V Forms/C. 2118/11.

Instructions regarding War Diaries and Intelligence Summaries are contained in F. S. Regs., Part II. and the Staff Manual respectively. Title pages will be prepared in manuscript.

WAR DIARY
~~or~~
~~INTELLIGENCE~~ SUMMARY.
(~~Erase heading not required.~~)

2nd SIGNAL SQUADRON No. .... Date .... 2nd CAVALRY DIVISION

Army Form C. 2118.

Hour, Date, Place		Summary of Events and Information	Remarks and references to Appendices
	1916		
THIEMBRONNE	Tues. Mar. 7th.	Sleet all day and then snow, which began to lie about 4 pm and by midnight 4" had fallen. Flag drill and pair work in the forenoon. Ditto afternoon buzzer reading and sending, lecture on the parts of the helio etc... Evening lecture on procedure. Counting etc. O.C. prepared report for submission to 2nd Army on the subject of cable wagons for Sig. Sqdn; and also discussed question of reorganization of signalling arrangements of 3rd Bde. RHA with C.RHA.	
	Wed. Mar. 8th.	Six inches of snow had fallen during the night, and the roads were in a bad state early. However the sun thawed it out a good deal during the day, but it froze after 6. pm. Buzzer Reading & Sending in the morning & lecture on the Message form. Ditto pm. and Flag drill. The glare from the sun on the snow was so bad that no reading work could be carried out. O.C. prepared and submitted proposals to G.S. for reorganization of communications of 3rd Bde. RHA. these being that the Artillery Bde. Comms: should be organized on exactly the same lines as a Bde. Signal Troop,	S.B. Capt

Instructions regarding War Diaries and Intelligence Summaries are contained in F. S. Regs., Part II. and the Staff Manual respectively. Title pages will be prepared in manuscript.

WAR DIARY

~~or~~

~~INTELLIGENCE SUMMARY~~.

(~~Erase heading not required.~~)

2nd SIGNAL SQUADRON No. .... Date .... 2nd CAVALRY DIVISION

Army Form C. 2118.

Hour, Date, Place		Summary of Events and Information	Remarks and references to Appendices
	1916.		
THIEMBRONNE	8/3/16. (contd.)	the Signal Officer being responsible to CRHA for the intercommunication, and to O.C. Signals on all technical matters, training, line laying, stores, etc....	
		Completed arrangements for Signal Course for Officers in the Division to commence at THIEMBRONNE on Ap. 1st.	
	Thurs. 9th March	Signallers station work am and pm. (close). Fine day all day.	
		O.C. saw signallers of 20th Hrs. and 5th Signal Troop under training in the afr.	
	Friday. 10th March	Snow and sleet early. Sigs. close station work am and pm.	
		O.C. saw signallers of Oxford Hrs. under training in the forenoon. This regt: having never had any signallers early in the war, a class is now being trained under 2 A.I.s found from the other 2 regts: in their Brigade.	
	Sat. 11th March.	Dull day. Thaw – and some drizzle. Sigs: station work etc...	
		VB put through to GHQ direct on D.C. set with 2 CO intermediates.	
	Sun. 12th March.	Usual Routine. Further thaw.	
	Mon: 13th March.	O.C. visited DDAS 2nd Army at Cassel on various matters – and saw 2nd Army Instrument Shops etc... Sigs. large flag drill + reading of thro telescope. Heavy thunderstorm 8 pm. but as precautions were taken no instruments were damaged.	F.W.B. Capt.

Instructions regarding War Diaries and Intelligence Summaries are contained in F. S. Regs., Part II. and the Staff Manual respectively. Title pages will be prepared in manuscript.

WAR DIARY

~~or~~

~~INTELLIGENCE SUMMARY.~~

(~~Erase heading not required.~~)

Army Form C. 2118.

2nd SIGNAL SQUADRON
No. ....
Date ....
2nd CAVALRY DIVISION

Hour, Date, Place	Summary of Events and Information	Remarks and references to Appendices
1916		
THIEMBRONNE. Tuesday. 14th Mar.	A very fine sunny day. Sigs. large flag drill, helio, flag through telescope, reading and sending etc.... Carried out tests of experimental pattern folding shutters and forwarded report on same.	
Wednesday. 15th Mar.	O.C. under orders from D.D.A.S. 2nd Army proceeded to Cassel to interview M.G.G.S. 2nd Army re subject of telephone for Cav. Regts. and Cable wagons for Sig. Sqdn. Drew stores from BAR.	
	Signallers Central station work done. Flag and shutters. Lamp by day etc.	
Thursday. 16th Mar.	Sigs flag drill & lamp by day am. and pm. distant station work – stations being 1 – 3 miles apart.	
	10 am Conference of Bde. and Regtl. Sig. Offrs. and issued instructions re labelling of lines, marking of equipment, faults noticed in training, usual procedure etc..	
	Orders having been received for the reorganization of 2nd Dismounted Bde for duty with 2nd Army if required. Had conference of Bde. Sig. Offrs. at 4.30 pm to discuss the establishment of the Bde. Signal Troop for this Bde.	[initials]

(9 29 6) W 2794 100,000 8/14 H W V Forms/C. 2118/11.

Instructions regarding War Diaries and Intelligence Summaries are contained in F. S. Regs., Part II. and the Staff Manual respectively. Title pages will be prepared in manuscript.

WAR DIARY

~~or~~

~~INTELLIGENCE SUMMARY.~~

(~~Erase heading not required.~~)

Army Form C. 2118.

Hour, Date, Place	Summary of Events and Information	Remarks and references to Appendices
1916		
THIEMBRONNE. Friday Mar. 17.	Sigs. Close station work. Foggy morning. p.m. Shutter & flag telescope reading. Issued Stores to Bdes. O.C. saw Signallers of 6: D.G. under training in the afternoon. Linemen disconnecting earthplates of telephone in the Division.	
Sat: Mar. 18.	Fine day but misty early. Long distance Station work in forenoon, stations being 2–5 miles apart. O.C. prepared and issued Establishment and Instructions for Dismounted Bde: Signal Troop. Linemen continued disconnection of earthplates.	
Sun: Mar. 19.	Usual Routine Church Parade etc.. O.C. visited D Battery RHA to discuss training of battery signallers etc...	
Mon. Mar 20.	Fine day but cloudy threatening, though only one slight shower fell. Signallers flag drill under Section leaders in forenoon. and Station work etc.. p.m. O.C visited and saw signallers of 4: Hussars and 5: Lancers in the forenoon. and 16 Lancers + 3: Sig: Tp. p.m.	
Tues: Mar. 21.	Completed disconnection of earthplates of telephones. Signallers buzzer reading and sending in the morning.	
Wed. Mar. 22.	Signallers Station work.	[initials]

Instructions regarding War Diaries and Intelligence Summaries are contained in F. S. Regs., Part II. and the Staff Manual respectively. Title pages will be prepared in manuscript.

WAR DIARY
or
~~INTELLIGENCE~~ SUMMARY.
(*Erase heading not required.*)

Army Form C. 2118.

Hour, Date, Place		Summary of Events and Information	Remarks and references to Appendices
	1916		
THIEMBRONNE	Thurs. Mar 23.	Buzzer & lecture on map Reading for Sigs.	
	Friday. Mar 24.	Sigs under training. Helio. flag telescope. buzzer etc.	
	Sat. Mar 25.	Sigs. Tests on all instruments. Reading and sending.	
	Sun: Mar 26.	Divl. Cav. of 2nd Army arrived in area for training. (3 Sqdns + Cyclist.)	
	Mon. Mar 27.	Sigs. Sending tests. & Station work.	
	Tues. Mar 28.	Snow on ground. Station work. Wet afternoon.	
	Wed. Mar 29.	Distant Visual Station work. Commenced construction of airline to 2nd Army Divl. Cav. Sqdns. building from ZCO exchange at LUMBRES to ACQUIN – BOUVELINGHEM – ALQUINES – HAUT LOQUIN.	
	Thurs. Mar 30.	Continued above line. (40 lb. bronze single comic airline.)	
	Fri. Mar. 31.	Completed this line & connected to ZCO exchange. 3 Sqdns. tied in with trench telephone. 15 officers joined the Squadron for Signal Course (6 weeks) commencing tomorrow. Lts. Rodney. Ashe. Cooper. R.S. Greys. Stretcher 12 L. Wordman. 20. H, Harris & Lavender. 3. H, Willis. 6. D.G. Smithson. 0x. H Buchanan and Castellain. 5. L. Mowbray & Thornton. 16. L. & Johnson 4. H. and Lt. Massy. (orderly offr. 3. Bde R.H.A.).	[signature] Capt.

(9 29 6) W 2794 100,000 8/14 H W V Forms/C. 2118/11.

Instructions regarding War Diaries and Intelligence Summaries are contained in F. S. Regs., Part II. and the Staff Manual respectively. Title pages will be prepared in manuscript.

WAR DIARY
~~or~~
~~INTELLIGENCE~~ SUMMARY.
(~~Erase heading not required.~~)

Army Form C. 2118.

Hour, Date, Place	Summary of Events and Information	Remarks and references to Appendices
1916.		
THEMBRONNE. Sat. April 1st.	Officers Signal Course commenced. & were tested on commencing.	
Sun. April 2nd.	Issued Supplementary Provisional Amendments to T.M.S.	
Mon. Ap. 3rd.	Offrs: Course visual Training. Sqdn: commenced cable training.	
	O.C. visited D.D.A.S. at Cassel. Drew stores etc.	
Tues. Ap. 4th.	Instruction and training as above.	
Wed. Ap. 5th.	Ditto. Installed 5-line exchange at Lumbres for Serving Railhead, Supply Clm, Hqrs: Sqdns. 2nd Army etc..	
Thurs. Ap. 6th.	O.C. visited O. i/c pigeon Service. G.H.Q. to discuss establishment of pigeon stations etc.. Diverted old ZCO-VC pair into THEMBRONNE to work to VBR at LUMBRES. Old ZCO-VB pair not working direct to SO. (for BAR).	
	ZCO Sigs. departed for WAILLY from LUMBRES.	
Fri. Ap. 7th.	Sqdn. carried out visual signalling scheme. Offrs. visual training.	
Sat. Ap. 8th.	Usual Routine and Training.	
Sun. Ap. 9th.	O.C. carried out line reconnaissances & inspections.	SWB
Mon. Ap. 10th.	Owing to proposed move to sea. O.C. reconnoitred for line near Coast	Capt.

Instructions regarding War Diaries and Intelligence Summaries are contained in F. S. Regs., Part II. and the Staff Manual respectively. Title pages will be prepared in manuscript.

WAR DIARY

~~or~~

~~INTELLIGENCE SUMMARY.~~

(~~Erase heading not required.~~)

Army Form C. 2118.

Hour, Date, Place	Summary of Events and Information	Remarks and references to Appendices
1916.		
THIEMBRONNE. Tues Ap. 11.	Bad weather. Rain and wind. Offrs.' Course commenced technical training. (Course of lectures by O.C.).	
Wed Ap. 12.	Very wet all day. Pigeon detachment rejoined from 2CD.	
Thurs. Ap. 13.	Offrs class. "Station work" visual. O.C. reconnoitred area about ACQUIN - BONNINGUES etc for lines in view of movement of regts. etc. to this area for training.	
Friday Ap. 14.	Installed 15-line exchange at VBR. Officers Course & Sqdn. carried out visual scheme at long distance. O.C. visited D.D.A.S. at CASSEL and arranged for lines in BONNINGUES area.	
Sat. Ap 15.	Installed 10 line exchange at VBR. & improved VBR office. Offrs. Course weekly examinations.	
Sun Ap 16.	Usual Routine.	
Mon. Ap 17.	Offrs Course Station and Central Station work etc.	
Tues Ap. 18.	Raining all day. Lectures etc.	
Wed. Ap. 19.	Ditto. Loaded pickets for tent pegs & carting from DRIONVILLE WOOD.	[illegible] Capt.

(9 29 6) W 2794 100,000 8/14 H W V Forms/C. 2118/11.

Army Form C. 2118.

Instructions regarding War Diaries and Intelligence Summaries are contained in F. S. Regs., Part II. and the Staff Manual respectively. Title pages will be prepared in manuscript.

WAR DIARY
or
INTELLIGENCE ~~SUMMARY~~.
(~~Erase heading not required.~~)

Hour, Date, Place	Summary of Events and Information	Remarks and references to Appendices
1916.		
THEMBRONNE, Thurs Ap. 20.	Showery day. Offrs: Course scheme "Moving Station Work" a.m. & in afternoon up till 10 pm. Advanced Station work in conjunction with the Sqdn.	
Friday Ap 21	Good Friday. Sunday Routine etc..	
Sat. Ap 22	Rained hard all day. Offrs. Class weekly exams etc..	
Sun. Ap 23.	Easter Sunday. Church Parade etc.. Sent 5 mounted Signalling instructors to 2nd Army Signal Training Camp at CASSEL for duty.	
Mon Ap. 24.	Fine day. Offrs Class commenced Cable Training. Sqdn: continuing cable training. O.C reconnoitred area LUMBRES–ALQUINES–REBERGUES–BONNINGUES etc.. for lines owing to impending changes in billeting areas of Bdes. etc..	
Tues. Ap 25th.	Fine day. Offrs. Signal Course cable and technical training.	
Wed. Ap 26.	Ditto. Ditto. Reeled up 3 line from VB–HERVARRE Chateau. O.C reconnoitred REBERGUES–ALQUINES–HARLETTES area for lines.	[illegible] Capt
Thurs. Ap 27.	Offrs. course continued cable & technical training.	

(9 29 6) W 2794 100,000 8/14 H W V Forms/C. 2118/11.

Instructions regarding War Diaries and Intelligence Summaries are contained in F.S. Regs., Part II. and the Staff Manual respectively. Title pages will be prepared in manuscript.

WAR DIARY

or

~~INTELLIGENCE SUMMARY.~~

(Erase heading not required.)

Army Form C. 2118.

Hour, Date, Place		Summary of Events and Information	Remarks and references to Appendices
1916			
THIEMBRONNE.	~~Friday~~ Ap. 28.	Fine day. Visual scheme all day. Offrs: course and Sqdn. Long distance O.C reconnoitred area BONNINGUES - GUEMY - LOUCHES - NORDAUSQUES etc. for lines.	
	Sat. Ap 29.	Offrs. course resumé of work. Instruction in field exchanges - and weekly examination (technical). Fine Day.	
	Sun. Ap 30.	Usual Routine. Fine day. Reeled up some spare & local lines.	
		30/4/16	
		[illegible] Captain	
		Cmdg Sigs.	2 Cav Div

(9 29 6) W 2794 100,000 8/14 H W V Forms/C. 2118/11.

2C

Army Form C. 2118.

Instructions regarding War Diaries and Intelligence Summaries are contained in F. S. Regs., Part II. and the Staff Manual respectively. Title pages will be prepared in manuscript.

WAR DIARY
or
~~INTELLIGENCE~~ SUMMARY.
(~~Erase heading not required.~~)

2nd SIGNAL SQUADRON No. .... Date .... 2nd CAVALRY DIVISION

May 1916.

Vol 10

Hour, Date, Place		Summary of Events and Information	Remarks and references to Appendices
	1916.		
THIEMBRONNE	Mon. May 1.	Fine day. Picked up spare pair of line MERCK J.P. — WAVRANS.	
		Officers class drawn in "Poled Cable" and lecture on D.I. & D.II Telephone.	
		HQ. 4 CB. moved to COLEMBERT. Pair PD on L. of C. Pairs 5 & 6. diverted. Superimposed through S.O. (intermediate)	
	Tues. May 2.	Fine am. another series of very heavy thunderstorms.	
		Constructed pair of line (Z.9. on S.P. B.&W. S-J. poles) from main NORDAUSQUES – BN road at GUEMY via LOUCHES to ~~AUDREHEM~~ AUTINGUES for connecting up PE when they move there.	
		Offrs. class laid 3 cable line to MERCK J-P.	
	Wed May 3.	Fine day. Reeled up cable line to FAUQUEMBERGUES; also cable line to WICQUAMETZ, also pair of Z.9. from YB to MERCK J-P.	
		Overhauled all Z.9 just picked up.	
		Offrs. Course instr: in Commutators, field exchanges. Fault finding on lines and instruments, jointing. Also lecture on C.2. Telephone.	
		5th Cav. Bde. moved to new area about BONNINGUES, TOURNEHEM. etc... with HQ. at Chateau SEPTFONTAINES close to AUTINGUES.	
		Put PE on with telephone across SO–PD pair for time.	
		Units of 4 CB. moved to about COLEMBERT etc.	[illegible signature]

(9 29 6) W 2794 100,000 8/14 H W V Forms/C. 2118/11.

Instructions regarding War Diaries and Intelligence Summaries are contained in F. S. Regs., Part II. and the Staff Manual respectively. Title pages will be prepared in manuscript.

WAR DIARY
or
INTELLIGENCE SUMMARY.
(*Erase heading not required.*)

2nd SIGNAL SQUADRON No. .... Date .... 2nd CAVALRY DIVISION

Army Form C. 2118.

Hour, Date, Place		Summary of Events and Information	Remarks and references to Appendices
	1916.		
THIEMBRONNE.	Thurs. May 4.	Officers class working in Squads. Men in Cable section. Office work. Same finding on lines and instruments. Fine day.	
		Reeled up cable section to NIELLES-LEZ-BLEQUIN.	
		Sent stores to LUMBRES. O.C. saw 2nd Army Comm. about drawing plans for new route in 2 Cav Div. Area.	
	Friday May 5th.	Officers class visual station work a.m. and visual work, flag drill etc... in evening.	
		O.C. carried out line reconnaissance about LUMBRES etc.	
LUMBRES.	Sat. May 6.	Div HQ. moved to LUMBRES. VB closed at THIEMBRONNE 8.30 a.m. and opened at LUMBRES same hour.	
		Offrs. Class reeled up the remaining lines to OUVE WIRQUIN.	
		PC came in with Morse in the VBR-VB pair, working down the line to VB at LUMBRES.	
		Signals constructed local lines, installing new Signal Office etc.	
	Sun. May 7.	All day spent in cleaning billets, work on local line, drawing stores from stations etc....	[initials] Capt.

(9 29 6) W 2794 100,000 8/14 H W V Forms/C. 2118/11.

Instructions regarding War Diaries and Intelligence Summaries are contained in F. S. Regs., Part II. and the Staff Manual respectively. Title pages will be prepared in manuscript.

WAR DIARY
~~or~~
~~INTELLIGENCE SUMMARY.~~
~~(Erase heading not required.)~~

Army Form C. 2118.

2nd SIGNAL SQUADRON * No. .... Date .... 2nd CAVALRY DIVISION *

Hour, Date, Place	Summary of Events and Information	Remarks and references to Appendices
1916.		
LUMBRES. Mon. May 8th.	Showery and wet day. Officers class built some - [illegible] for 4th Cav Bde from BOIS ROBLIN to ESCOEUILLES. In evening lecture on "Line & Telephones" and "Systematic Testing of Instruments".	
	Commenced construction of new 4-line route LUMBRES – HARLETTES – HAUT LOQUIN – REBERGUES. (20 ft. [illegible] poles, P.O. insulators, and 40-lb bronze with a 4-way arm.) Erected poles to NW of BAYENGHEM.	
	D.D.A.S. 2nd Army visited O.C. and discussed certain questions.	
Tues. May 9th.	Very wet day. Continued REBERGUES route.	
	Officers Class weekly Exams on Telephones etc. Lecture on "Vibrator". Practice in testing instruments etc. - - -	
Wed. May 10th.	Fine day. Continued REBERGUES route. Offrs. Class lecture on "Morse System" and further [illegible] in office procedure, fault finding etc. - - -	
	In afternoon Maj. WILLAN. A.D.A.S. Canadian Corps came down and gave a lecture on "Trench Communications". This lecture was attended by Offrs. class, all Signal Offrs. in the division, and N.C.O.s and men of Signal units, Sqdn, Sig. [illegible] etc. - - -	[signature]

(9 29 6) W 2791 100,000 8/14 H W V Forms/C. 2118/11.

Instructions regarding War Diaries and Intelligence Summaries are contained in F. S. Regs., Part II. and the Staff Manual respectively. Title pages will be prepared in manuscript.

WAR DIARY
or
~~INTELLIGENCE SUMMARY.~~
(Erase heading not required.)

Army Form C. 2118.

Hour, Date, Place	Summary of Events and Information	Remarks and references to Appendices
1916		
LUMBRES. Thurs. May 11.	Fine day. Offrs. class went out by lorry to trenches in Training Area near PETIT DIFQUES — and practised burying cable — pegging cable into trenches etc... till 4 pm.	
	In evening Lt. JOHNSON. 2nd Army Signals came down and lectured on the "Fullerphone". This lecture was attended by Offrs. class, all Signal officers etc.... & a practical demonstration of the uses of the instrument was given. Continued REBERGUES route.	
Friday. May 12.	Continued REBERGUES route.	
	Offrs. class lecture on "Superimposing, Transformers etc.." and the "handling of Bde: Signal Troop on the march".	
	Col. Hildebrand D.D.A.S. 2nd Army came down and gave a lecture on "Progress of Communications" – which was attended by all Signal officers.	
Sat. May 13.	A Bde. Scheme was to have taken place — and the Sqdn paraded at 6 am to take part in it — but owing to it being a very wet morning the scheme was cancelled.	
	Offrs class fault-finding on line instrument (final test). Continued REBERGUES route.	F.W.B. Capt.

Instructions regarding War Diaries and Intelligence Summaries are contained in F. S. Regs., Part II. and the Staff Manual respectively. Title pages will be prepared in manuscript.

WAR DIARY
or
INTELLIGENCE SUMMARY.
(*Erase heading not required.*)

Army Form C. 2118.

Hour, Date, Place		Summary of Events and Information	Remarks and references to Appendices
	1916.		
LUMBRES.	Sun. May 14.	Fine day. Continued REBERGUES route.	
	Mon May 15.	Wet day. Completed poling of REBERGUES route. O.C. inspected line VB – WISQUES, WIZERNES, ESQUERDES etc.	
		Offrs. class final tests in cable laying, testing instruments etc. and in the evening final written paper on "Visual Procedure".	
	Tues May 16.	Fine day. Offrs class final technical exam. a.m. and in afternoon and evening they were tested in "Knowledge of Visual Instruments" and "Giving 5-minute lectures on any subject dealt with during the course." This completed the course.	
		O.C. inspected VA Morse line to LEDINGHEM – and reconnoitred for route for poles to Field Sqdn: at LEDINGHEM.	
		Adjusted and strengthened completed portion of REBERGUES route.	
		O.C. lectured operators on "The Fullerphone" at 9.30 pm.	
	Wed. May 17.	O.C. reconnoitred "Training Area" for visual stations. Fine day.	
		O.i/c. line 2nd Army came down and was shown all lines in VB system including new route under construction. Cable Sect. from BAR arrived to be attached for line construction work.	[illegible]
		31 RHA Signallers from the Divn: joined for a month's signalling course.	

Instructions regarding War Diaries and Intelligence Summaries are contained in F. S. Regs., Part II. and the Staff Manual respectively. Title pages will be prepared in manuscript.

WAR DIARY
or
INTELLIGENCE SUMMARY.
(Erase heading not required.)

Army Form C. 2118.

2nd SIGNAL SQUADRON * No.......... Date.......... 2nd CAVALRY DIVISION

Hour, Date, Place	Summary of Events and Information	Remarks and references to Appendices
1916		
LUMBRES. Thurs. May 18th.	Fine day. Officers Signal Class left at 9.30 am by lorry for HQ 2nd Army. Where officers were distributed to divisions in the line for a week's attachment to learn signal work.	
	R.H.A. class commenced usual training under Lt BRAND.	
	Cable Section under Lt HARRIS commenced reconstruction of 5-line route LUMBRES - SETQUES. Continued REBERGUES route.	
Friday May 19.	Fine Day. Divisional Scheme in Training Area. Inspected by Gen. Sir H GOUGH. Scheme carried out was "gap scheme" by 5th CB. Other Bdes. & Div HQ represented by signal units & one staff officer in order to practise intercommunication. Helios were much used and with considerable success.	
Sat. May 20th.	Fine day. Completed 4-line route to REBERGUES. O.C. visited 5th Sig Tp. stuck on motorcycle [illegible]. Cable section continued reconstruction of SETQUES route.	
Sun. May 21.	Usual Routine. Church Parade etc.	
	Adjusted REBERGUES route. Crossing lines at 4 places etc....	[initials] Capt

(9 29 6) W 2794 100,000 8/14 H W V Forms/C. 2118/11.

Instructions regarding War Diaries and Intelligence Summaries are contained in F. S. Regs., Part II. and the Staff Manual respectively. Title Pages will be prepared in manuscript.

1916

WAR DIARY

~~or~~

~~INTELLIGENCE SUMMARY~~

~~(Erase heading not required.)~~

Army Form C. 2118.

Place	Date MAY.	~~Hour~~	Summary of Events and Information	Remarks and references to Appendices
LUMBRES.	22nd	Mon:	V. Hot day. Some showers. RHA & Linemen's classes usual instruction. Completed reconstruction of JETQVES route. Continued adjusting local wiring in LUMBRES.	
	23rd	Tues.	4th Cav. Bde carried out scheme in Training area. All Signal units took part. Helio largely used. Visual work good throughout. Changed over 3D and WIZERNES line onto new JETQVES route — and changed over Poles onto new REBERGUES route. Pulled up old JETQVES 5-line route. Promulgated results of Offrs: Signalling Course and issued Signalling certificates.	
	24th	Wed.	Classes under instruction etc... Offrs. Signal course returned from attachment to Divns of 2nd Army, and rejoined their Regts. Commenced construction of new pair to LEDINGHEM (2nd Field Sqdn:) via St PIERRE.	
	25th	Thurs.	Continued LEDINGHEM route. Preliminary day of Divl: Horseshow.	
	26.	Friday.	Usual Routine. Classes under instruction etc... Completed wiring through the Town which was a difficult matter owing to the indiscriminate way in which the civilian lighting circuits are run — and their installation.	
	27th	Sat:	Divl: Horse Show. Whole holiday in the Divn.	
	28th	Sun.	Usual Routine. Church Parade etc... Carried up poles etc.. for LEDINGHEM route.	[initials] Capt.

2449 Wt. W14957/M90 750,000 1/16 J.B.C. & A. Forms/C.2118/12.

Army Form C. 2118.

WAR DIARY
~~or~~ ~~INTELLIGENCE SUMMARY~~
(Erase heading not required.)

Instructions regarding War Diaries and Intelligence Summaries are contained in F. S. Regs., Part II. and the Staff Manual respectively. Title Pages will be prepared in manuscript.

1916.

Place	Date MAY	Hour	Summary of Events and Information	Remarks and references to Appendices
LUMBRES	29.	Mon.	Fine day. Gap scheme by 3rd Cav Bde. in Training area — attended by all Signal units. Visual used for practically all communication. All Signal units attended this scheme. RDA and linemen's course usual run. Wire up LEDINGHEM route to St PIERRE.	
	30.	Tues.	Very wet morning. but cleared into fine day after 10 am. O.C with 15 men continued LEDINGHEM line. poling and wiring to 1' S.W. of St PIERRE. Classes under men as usual.	
	31.	Wed.	O.C with 15 men continued LEDINGHEM route and built up to THEROUANNE – BOULOGNE road at BOIS DE THIEMBRONNE. Lt. Adams with 2nd Army Airline Sec. poled same route from LE MESNIL to LEDINGHEM. 10-days linemen course completed. All linemen tested for rating as "F.L.T. (proficient)". 8 out of 11 were passed for ..., the other 3 failed. Sgt. CHRISTIAN of Pigeon Service arrived from GHQ for 3 days as instructor for pigeon-flying course. Very fine day.	

[signature]
Captain.
Comdg. Signals, 2nd Cavalry Division.

1st June 1916

Instructions regarding War Diaries and Intelligence Summaries are contained in F. S. Regs., Part II. and the Staff Manual respectively. Title Pages will be prepared in manuscript.

1916

~~WAR DIARY~~ or INTELLIGENCE ~~SUMMARY~~

(Erase heading not required.)

June 1916.

Army Form C. 2118.

2 C

Vol XI

Place	Date JUNE	Hour	Summary of Events and Information	Remarks and references to Appendices
LUMBRES	1	Thurs.	Pigeon Flying Course commenced – 2 men from each troop and 10 from Sig. Sqdn. Birds were fetched from lofts at St OMER and instruction given in handling – message writing – feeding – etc.... Completed line to Field Sqdn. at LEDINGHEM. News received of Battle of JUTLAND. Completed labelling and adjusting of all lines. RHA class continued visual training.	
	2	Friday.	Pigeon flying course continued – class working in 2 parties a.m. & p.m. – one party dispatching birds from LUMBRES and the other party receiving them at the lofts at St OMER. O.C. went to CASSEL for conference of Signal Officers under D.D.A.S. 2nd Army. Germans attacked on front of Canadian Corps from HOOGE to OBSERVATORY RIDGE. RHA class continued visual training.	
	3	Sat.	3rd M/G Sqdn. moved up to KEMMEL defences for duty there. Fine day. Pigeon course concluded with instruction in the use of the French Cavalry Pigeon basket – & further instruction in the care of birds – feeding etc....	
	4	Sun.	Windy day & wet p.m. O.C. visited O.C. 1st Sig. Sqdn. to discuss signal questions.	
	5	Mon.	Wet & windy. Inspection of arms – equipment – bicycles – & saddles. O.C. working on improved pattern of the Service electric lamp – reducing it to a size suitable for portability for cavalry work.	

[illegible]

Instructions regarding War Diaries and Intelligence Summaries are contained in F. S. Regs., Part II. and the Staff Manual respectively. Title Pages will be prepared in manuscript.

WAR DIARY
~~or~~
~~INTELLIGENCE SUMMARY~~

(Erase heading not required.)

Army Form C. 2118.

2nd SIGNAL SQUADRON
No. ....
Date ....
2nd CAVALRY DIVISION

Place	Date JUNE	Hour	Summary of Events and Information	Remarks and references to Appendices
LUMBRES	6.	Tues.	Wet and windy. Reeled up the SO-YA morse line from SENLECQUES - DESVRES road to MENNES-LEZ-BLEQUIN. This line being now out of use and in bad repair. Cleaned up and sorted all stores. 2nd Div Bde ordered to be held in readiness to move at short notice. This order was cancelled about 5 pm. Heard of great Russian offensive from PRIPET to ROUMANIA. with 25000 prisoners first day.	
	7.	Wed.	Wet morning - clearing later. Continued to recover the SO-YA morse line & packed up section from MENNES-LEZ-BLEQUIN to 1 mile W of LUMBRES. O.C. Lt. Brand & S.M. etc... attended C.M at OUVE WIRQUIN. 2nd Div. Bde. was ordered to be embussed in the forenoon and left at 5 pm by motor bus for RENINGHELST. where it came under Canadian Corps in Corps Reserve. Composite Sig. Tp was assembled and sent to RENINGHELST in command of Lt. A.R. BODEN (3 Sig. Tp.). Brig. Gen. Campbell (S.C.B) in command of 2 Div. Bde. The RHA. Field Sqdn. and Amm: Col. did not go with Div. Bde. Heard of the death of Lord Kitchener. Sent Lt. Moore (4 Sig. Tp) to KEMMEL defences on liaison as regards the communications existing and required for our working party there.	AB Capt

Instructions regarding War Diaries and Intelligence Summaries are contained in F. S. Regs., Part II. and the Staff Manual respectively. Title Pages will be prepared in manuscript.

WAR DIARY
~~or~~
~~INTELLIGENCE SUMMARY~~
(Erase ~~heading not required.~~)

Army Form C. 2118.

Place	Date JUNE	Hour	Summary of Events and Information	Remarks and references to Appendices
LUMBRES	8th	Thurs.	Fine day. Experts from 2 Army inspected and tested all motorcycles of signal units in the division. R.H.A. class last day of visual instruction. Russians now have 41,000 prisoners and 270 guns.	
	9th	Friday	Fine day. RHA class visual tests and written exam. paper. Russians 51.000 prisoners	
	10th	Sat.	Stormy day and a good deal of rain. RHA class concluded visual tests – and classification showed out of the 31 trained:– 1st class 22 N.C.O. and men. 2nd class 5 do. Failed 2 do.	
	11th	Sun.	Fairly fine – but very heavy thunderstorm just before 1 pm. O.C. visited D.D.A.S. at Cassel, + took up experimental electric – signalling lamps.	
	12th	Mon.	Wet + windy. RHA class commenced cable training. Russians have 107 000 prisoners	
	13.	Tues.	Wet day all day and stormy last. Owing to orders being received for H.Q. 3rd Bde RHA + E. + J. Batteries to be held in readiness to proceed to Canadian Corps – the cable training of the signallers of these units had to be abandoned + they rejoined their units. Sigs. J.D. Battery however continued training. Canadians [illegible] OBSERVATORY ridge. Russians have got 114 000 prisoners.	[illegible] Capt

2449 Wt. W14957/M90 750,000 1/16 J.B.C. & A. Forms/C.2118/12.

Army Form C. 2118.

WAR DIARY
or
~~INTELLIGENCE SUMMARY~~
(Erase heading not required.)

Instructions regarding War Diaries and Intelligence Summaries are contained in F. S. Regs., Part II. and the Staff Manual respectively. Title Pages will be prepared in manuscript.

1916

Place	Date JUNE	Hour	Summary of Events and Information	Remarks and references to Appendices
LUMBRES	14.	Wed.	Usual Routine. HQ 3rd Bde RHA E & J Batteries marched to join Canadian Corps Reserve.	
	15.	Thurs.	After a wet night it was fairly fine. Usual Routine. Russians now have 123.000 prisoners.	
	16.	Friday.	Weather cleared into fine day. O.C. visited 4th Sig. Tp. Russians 152.000 prisoners.	
	17.	Sat.	Fine day. O.C. visited D.D.A.S. at Cassel. Continued work of adapting service lamps in accordance with our new design.	
	18.	Sun.	Fine. 3rd Dis. Bn. returned from Cav: Corps. Kemmel defences working party also returned. Owing to impending movements the Sigs: J.D.(?) Battery broke off their cable training and rejoined their Battery.	
	19.	Mon.	Overcast but no rain. 4th Dis. Bn. returned from Cav. Corps. 3rd Cav. Bde. marched at dawn to area about STRAZEELE. Sent party to reconnoitre lines handed over to us by BAR to erect(?) poles in new area about HAZEBROUCK. Returned surplus stores to Signal Park and some to 2nd Army Signal Comp. 6 men reported from W.T. course at BAR. Dis. Bde. Sig. Tp. returned. Horse inspection 9.30 am.	
	20.	Tues.	Fine day. 5th Dis. Bn. returned from Cav: Corps. 4th Cav. Bde marched at 7 pm. to intermediate area about EBBLINGHEM. Rearguard(?) moved to HAZEBROUCK.	Sm/Capt

2449 Wt. W14957/M90 750,000 1/16 J.B.C. & A. Forms/C.2118/12.

Instructions regarding War Diaries and Intelligence Summaries are contained in F. S. Regs., Part II. and the Staff Manual respectively. Title Pages will be prepared in manuscript.

1916.

WAR DIARY
or
~~INTELLIGENCE SUMMARY~~

(Erase heading not required.)

2nd Signal Squadron ... Cavalry Division

Army Form C. 2118.

Place	Date	Hour	Summary of Events and Information	Remarks and references to Appendices
LUMBRES.	21.	Wed.	Fine day. 5th Cav. Bde marched at 7 pm to EBBLINGHEM area. 4th Cav. Bde vacated their area at 7 pm and marched to MONT DOULIEU and NEUF BERQUIN. 7. Sqdn. to AU SOUVERAIN. Amm. Pk to HK. Amm Col. to BORRES etc. Completed mobilization of light signalling equipment for mobile operations.	
	22.	Thurs.	Fine day. Remaining units moved to HK area.	
HAZEBROUCK.			Div Report Centre closed at LUMBRES 5 pm. and reopened at HK Town Hall. Sqdn: marched at 9. am. to HK. via REMINT WIRQUIN – INGHEM – ECQUES – CORVETOIRE and SERCUS. Advanced party (car & m/cs) under Lt Coutts left at 8 am. to install new office.	
	23.	Friday	Usual Routine. Continued work on electric signalling lamps, getting use of 2nd Army Workshops for the purpose, and installing the Sqdn: instrument repairer there to work.	
	24.	Sat.	Usual Routine. O.C. visited all Bdes.	
	25.	Sun.	Usual Routine. Church Parade etc.	
	26.	Mon.	Fine day. 9th Lr. Armd: Car: Battery left the Div: to join 2nd Indian Cav. Div.	
	27.	Tues.		
	28.	Wed.	Division in readiness to move at 6 hrs. notice either mounted or dismounted to support any	
	29.	Thurs.	part of either 1st or 2nd Army as required – being held as G.H.Q. Reserve.	
	30.	Friday		

[signature] Captain.
Cmdg Signals 2nd Cavalry Division.

2449 Wt. W14957/M90 750,000 1/16 J.B.C. & A. Forms/C.2118/12.

Vol XII

CONFIDENTIAL.

WAR DIARY

of

2nd Signal Squadron. R.E.

from: 1st July to: 31st July. 1916.

(Volume XXIII.).

Instructions regarding War Diaries and Intelligence Summaries are contained in F. S. Regs., Part II. and the Staff Manual respectively. Title Pages will be prepared in manuscript.

1916.

WAR DIARY
or
~~INTELLIGENCE SUMMARY~~
(Erase heading not required.)

Army Form C. 2118.

2nd SIGNAL SQUADRON · No. .... Date .... · 2nd CAVALRY DIVISION

Place	Date JULY	Hour	Summary of Events and Information	Remarks and references to Appendices
HAZEBROUCK.	1st.	Sat.	This day. British and French offensive commenced N. & S. of the SOMME. Div: in readiness to move at 6 hrs. notice – (G.H.Q. reserve) – with mounted [illegible] detachments – to support any part of 1st or 2nd Armies.	
	2nd.	Sun.	Usual Routine. Church Parade etc. Sqdn: turned out in active service order. [illegible]	
	3rd.	Mon.	Usual Routine.	
	4th	Tues	Usual Routine.	
	5th	Weds	Usual Routine. Sent a lorry down to LUMBRES a few airline stores in case of emergency.	
	6th	Thurs	Usual Routine. Sqdn did some flag drill from 2.15 PM to 4.15 P.M.	
	7th	Fri	Usual Routine. 2nd Lieut G.S. Courtney R.E. is struck off the strength & posted to 3rd SIGNAL TROOP	
	8th	Sat	Lieut A.P. BODEN XII ROYAL LANCERS attd 3rd SIGNAL TROOP is posted to SIGNALS 9th CORPS. LIEUT F. THORNTON 16th Lancers joined VB temporarily for duty vice 2nd LT COURTNEY.	
	9th	Sun	Church Parade: 3rd Bde move to WALLON CAPPELL. Put up new derrick pole in chateau grounds & rewired from VB office to HK.	
	10th	Mon	Brought up D.C. set & test-board from LUMBRES & installed them in VB office. Finished off rewiring to HK & joined up test-board. All Bdes were put on the morse to-day.	
	11th	Tues	Usual routine. Sqdn did flag drill from 2.15 – 4.15 PM.	
	12th	Weds	Usual routine. Capt. French Blake ~~left~~ left for England to report to W.D. preparatory to proceeding to EGYPT	[initials]

2449 Wt. W14957/M90 750,000 1/16 J.B.C. & A. Forms/C.2118/12.

Instructions regarding War Diaries and Intelligence Summaries are contained in F. S. Regs., Part II. and the Staff Manual respectively. Title Pages will be prepared in manuscript.

WAR DIARY
or
INTELLIGENCE SUMMARY

(Erase heading not required.)

Army Form C. 2118.

2nd SIGNAL SQUADRON
No. ....
Date ....
2nd CAVALRY DIVISION

Place	Date July	Hour	Summary of Events and Information	Remarks and references to Appendices
HAZEBRUCK	13th	Thurs.	Usual Routine. Sqdn did close station work from 2.15 to 4.15 PM. 2nd Lt H.J. LEVANDER 3rd HUSSARS joined for duty. 2nd Lt W. DARLING ROYAL SCOTS GREYS joined on probation.	
	14th	Fri.	Usual Routine. Sqdn did close station work from 2.15 to 4.15 P.M. 2nd Lt DARLING under instruction with SGT EGAN	
	15th	Sat.	3rd Bde move to MERRIS and have to come off the wires. 4th Bde move to BLEU. Cabled 4th Bde through temporarily from VIEUX BIRQUIN to BLEU. Sqdn did stn work in the afternoon.	
	16th	Sun.	Church Parade. Changed cable to BLEU over to airline. Picked up stores from HUMBRES for the purpose.	
	17th	Mon.	Usual Routine. Close stn work in the afternoon. DDAS 2nd ARMY visited HQ. Reinforcement 3 telephonists arrived at 5 P.M.	
	18th	Tues.	Usual Routine. Close stn work in the afternoon. m/c Cpl North from Divl. Rest Station.	
	19th	Weds.	Usual Routine. Signalling in the afternoon.	
	20th	Thurs	Usual Routine. Signalling in the afternoon.	
	21st	Fri.	Usual Routine. Signalling in the afternoon. Sprs BOWES and CLARKE to 2nd Army Sigs. 2nd LT DARLING and 2 servants returned to their regt.	
	22nd	Sat.	Usual Routine	
	23rd	Sun.	Usual Routine. Church Parade	[initials]

2449 Wt. W14957/M90 750,000 1/16 J.B.C. & A. Forms/C.2118/12.

Instructions regarding War Diaries and Intelligence Summaries are contained in F. S. Regs., Part II. and the Staff Manual respectively. Title Pages will be prepared in manuscript.

WAR DIARY
or
INTELLIGENCE SUMMARY
(Erase heading not required.)

2nd SIGNAL SQDN. No. ...... Date ...... 2nd CAVALRY DIVISION

Army Form C. 2118.

Place	Date July	Hour	Summary of Events and Information	Remarks and references to Appendices
HAZEBRUCK	24th	Mon	Usual Routine. Spr GRANT transferred to PD. Spr COBB transferred from PD to VS. Spr COOPER joined from BASE.	
	25th	Tues	Usual Routine. Semaphore Signalling 2.15 till 4.15.	
	26th	Weds	Usual Routine. Semaphore Signalling 2.15 till 4.15.	
	27th	Thurs	Usual Routine. Test for Signal linemen commenced. Lamps 9.30 pm till 10.30	
	28th	Fri	Usual Routine. Test for Signal linemen concluded. All passed.	
	29th	Sat	Usual Routine. Pnr PEACH to Divl Rest Stn.	
	30th	Sun	Usual Routine. Church parade etc. Pnr PEACH evacuated to Hospital. O.C. went to BAR to see about new lines to 4th BDE	
	31st	Mon	4th BDE move to BORRE. O.C. went to STRAZEELE and put RYx8 through to SAXH, so getting 4th BDE direct on the move.	

1st August 1916

[signature] O.C. Signals 2nd Cav: Div:

2449 Wt. W14957/M90 750,000 1/16 J.B.C. & A. Forms/C.2118/12.

Vol 13

CONFIDENTIAL.

WAR DIARY OF

2nd SIGNAL SQUADRON

for August, 1916.

Vol XXII

Instructions regarding War Diaries and Intelligence Summaries are contained in F. S. Regs., Part II. and the Staff Manual respectively. Title Pages will be prepared in manuscript.

WAR DIARY
or
~~INTELLIGENCE SUMMARY~~

(Erase heading not required.)

Army Form C. 2118.

2nd SIGNAL SQUADRON
No. ....
Date ....
2nd CAVALRY DIVISION

Place	Date	Hour	Summary of Events and Information	Remarks and references to Appendices
	Aug			
HAZEBRUCK	1st	Tues	Usual Routine. 'A' Section and all linemen under 2nd LT LEVANDER reeled up air-line from VIEUX BERQUIN to BLEU. O.C. took LT CODRINGTON to BAR to see DDAS. Pnr KEMP joined	
	2nd	Wed	Sent up to BAR and fetched two Fullerphones. Sent Sgt Melton over to 5th Bde to explain working of Fullerphone. O.C. visited PC to test 3 men for Signaller linemen.	
	3rd	Thurs	Put through HB 14 & 15 to P.C. thereby getting them direct on the Morse. O.C. visited PC and tested Sgt HARRISON 5th Lancers and SGT SHORT 16th Lancers as Assistant Instructors	
	4th	Fri	O.C. visited 5th Bde and tested 6 men for Signaller Linemen. Usual Routine with Sqdn. Signalling in the afternoon. Dr Smith to Divl Rest Stn: Sick	
	5th	Sat	Usual Routine. 4 more Working Parties left the Divn.	
	6th	Sun	Usual Routine. Church Parade etc	
	7th	Mon	Usual Routine. Installed 15 line exchange and started converting 10 line exchange into an exchange 10 line ringing and 5 line buzzer.	
	8th	Tues.	Usual Routine. Commenced to build a line to SUPPLY COLUMN and ORHA. L/Cpl LANE and PNR MURRAY to DIVL REST STN	
	9th	Weds	Completed line to SUPPLY COLUMN and CRHA and put both on the telephone. In the afternoon put the O.C. ASC on the telephone.	
	10th	Thurs	O.C. visited 3 MG Det and made arrangements about their being on the telephone. 2/Lt LEVANDER put Nos Mess on the telephone.	
	11th	Fri	Usual Routine. Sent out and put 4th M.G. Det. on to CAESTRE exchange.	[signature]

2449 Wt. W14957/M90 750,000 1/16 J.B.C. & A. Forms/C.2118/12.

Instructions regarding War Diaries and Intelligence Summaries are contained in F. S. Regs., Part II. and the Staff Manual respectively. Title Pages will be prepared in manuscript.

WAR DIARY
or
INTELLIGENCE SUMMARY

(Erase heading not required.)

Army Form C. 2118.

Place	Date Aug	Hour	Summary of Events and Information	Remarks and references to Appendices
HAZEBRUCK	13	Sun	Routine as usual. Church parade etc.	
	14	Mon	Usual Routine. Signalling in the afternoon. Pnr MURRAY evacuated sick.	
	15	Tues	Usual Routine. Signalling in the afternoon	
	16	Weds	Usual Routine. Signalling as usual. Spr MANDER to 5th SIG TROOP Spr BLAKE joined from 5th SIG TROOP.	
	17	Thurs	Usual Routine. Saddle inspection 3 p.m. Inspection of bicycles, motor bicycles etc 3.30 p.m. Arms inspection 4 p.m. Received 22 telephone cases for completing VB pattern lamp this day	
	18	Fri	Usual Routine. Instrument repairers proceeded with work on VB pattern lamp. L/Cpl WESTLAKE instructed 'A' Section in jointing cable. O.C. visited DDAS and got use of mule pack winding gear.	
	19	Sat	Usual Routine. L/Cpl WESTLAKE instructed 'B' Section in jointing cable. A/Sgt MAIN left for V.C.	
	20	Sun	Usual Routine. Church parade under Sgt EGAN.	
	21	Mon	Usual Routine. L/Cpl WESTLAKE instructed 'D' Section in jointing cable.	
	22	Tues	Usual Routine. L/Cpl WESTLAKE instructed 'C' Section in jointing cable.	
	23	Wed	Usual Routine. L/Cpl WESTLAKE instructed 4 men 3rd SIG. TROOP in jointing cable. Visited Capt WESTON B.A.R. ref lines in new area. Capt DIGGLE 9th LANCERS having joined to-day is taken on the strength. Ptes ANDREWS & REID joined this day.	[illegible signature]

Army Form C. 2118.

WAR DIARY
or
INTELLIGENCE SUMMARY

(Erase heading not required.)

Instructions regarding War Diaries and Intelligence Summaries are contained in F. S. Regs., Part II. and the Staff Manual respectively. Title Pages will be prepared in manuscript.

2nd SIGNAL SQUADRON No.......... Date.......... 2nd CAVALRY DIVISION

Place	Date Aug.	Hour	Summary of Events and Information	Remarks and references to Appendices
HAZEBRUCK	24th	Thurs	L/Cpl. Westlake instructed 4 men of 4th Sig Troop in jointing cable.	
"	25th	Fri.	L/Cpl. Westlake instructed 4 men of 5th Sig Troop in jointing cable.	
"	26th	Sat.	Orders issued for a signal Officer to mount at 6p.m. daily & take over the signal office for 24 hours. Lieut Brand & 15 N.C.Os & men left for Lumbres by lorry to pick up lines built in the neighbourhood with a view to using the stores in the new billeting area. Owing to an alteration of billeting areas in the back area all arrangements with Sigs BAR to build lines were cancelled.	
"	27th	Sun	Nothing to report	
"	28th	Mon	Party continued picking up old lines round Lumbres. New system of registering telegrams introduced	
"	29th	Tues.	Party picking up lines at Lumbres.	

2449 Wt. W14957/M90 750,000 1/16 J.B.C. & A. Forms/C.2118/12.

Instructions regarding War Diaries and Intelligence Summaries are contained in F. S. Regs., Part II. and the Staff Manual respectively. Title Pages will be prepared in manuscript.

WAR DIARY
or
~~INTELLIGENCE SUMMARY~~
(Erase heading not required.)

2nd SIGNAL SQUADRON · No. .... Date .... · 2nd CAVALRY DIVISION

Army Form C. 2118.

Place	Date	Hour	Summary of Events and Information	Remarks and references to Appendices
HAZEBROUCK	30th	✓	Party at Lumbres commenced a pair from COLEMBERT to ALINETHUM.	
"	31st	✓	Billeting arrangements round COLEMBERT having been cancelled the party under Lieut BRAND returned	

J.W. Digg[?] Capt
9th Lancers
Cmdg 2nd Signal Squadron

2449 Wt. W14957/M90 750,000 1/16 J.B.C. & A. Forms/C.2118/12.

Vol 13

S E C R E T.

WAR DIARY

of

2nd SIGNAL SQUADRON

for September, 1916.

====

VOLUME [illegible].

****

Instructions regarding War Diaries and Intelligence Summaries are contained in F. S. Regs., Part II. and the Staff Manual respectively. Title Pages will be prepared in manuscript.

WAR DIARY
or
~~INTELLIGENCE SUMMARY~~
(Erase heading not required.)

Army Form C. 2118.

Place	Date	Hour	Summary of Events and Information	Remarks and references to Appendices
HAZEBROUCK.	1st Sept.		Nothing to report.	
"	2nd "		New pack cable horse tested. The working parties & machine gun squadrons were withdrawn. The latter & left their instruments installed & new ones were issued by the 2nd Army to replace them	
"	3rd		Nothing to report.	
"	4th		Nothing to report.	
"	5th		Nothing to report.	
"	6th		The division moved to ST. VENANT 2pm. The brigades were disposed as follows:—	
St. Venant		2pm	PC —— ROBECQ. PD —— BURBURE PE —— ALLOUAGNE RHA —— BUSNES. Communication to them was by DR. Full circuits shown in appendix I ½ a lorry load of stores were taken by Supply Column forces. The remainder were returned to 2nd Army.	Appendix I
MONCHY CAYEUX	7th	2pm	The St. Venant office closed at 2pm. An office was opened at MONCHY CAYEUX the same time. All the circuits are shown in appendix II. Capt. James RFC & 7 ORs RFC joined the unit with Wireless, a tender & necessary stores.	App II

2449 Wt. W14957/M90 750,000 1/16 J.B.C. & A. Forms/C.2118/12.

Instructions regarding War Diaries and Intelligence Summaries are contained in F. S. Regs., Part II. and the Staff Manual respectively. Title Pages will be prepared in manuscript.

WAR DIARY
or
INTELLIGENCE SUMMARY
(Erase heading not required.)

Army Form C. 2118.

Place	Date	Hour	Summary of Events and Information	Remarks and references to Appendices
Willeman	Sept. 8th	11am	The office at MONCHY CAYEUX closed at 11 am. An office was opened at the same time at WILLEMAN. As the village selected for Div. Hqrs had no lines to it & the DDAS III Army had already pointed this out the DDAS did not build any line to us. However a pair of cables was subsequently laid from HESDIN on which we subsequently superimposed. The cables however were not laid till after our arrival. Full circuits are shown in Appendix III.	App III
			The[re] was a conference at ZCO of all 5 signal sqdn commanders.	
WILLEMAN	Sept. 9th		The Div did not move. Wagons were re-packed & a general overhaul made.	
FROHEN LE GRAND	Sept 10.	11am	The office at WILLEMAN closed at 11 am. & reopened the same hour at FROHEN LE GRAND. A pair of lines to DOULLENS civil were handed over to us. These we superimposed on as shown in App. IV.	App IV
VIGNACOURT	Sept. 11	11am	Office at FROHEN LE GRAND closed 11 am. reopened at VIGNACOURT same hour. Telegraph messages were ~~to~~ sent to an office of the 10th Corps at VIGNACOURT. Telephone circuits were as shown in Appendix V.	App V
			At FROHEN LE GRAND I was informed that the mounted DRs I was told would be attached to the sqdn. would not be given to me.	

2449 Wt. W14957/M90 750,000 1/16 J.B.C. & A. Forms/C.2118/12.

Instructions regarding War Diaries and Intelligence Summaries are contained in F. S. Regs., Part II. and the Staff Manual respectively. Title Pages will be prepared in manuscript.

WAR DIARY
or
INTELLIGENCE SUMMARY
(Erase heading not required.)

Army Form C. 2118.

2nd SIGNAL SQUADRON No. .... Date .... 2nd CAVALRY DIVISION

Place	Date	Hour	Summary of Events and Information	Remarks and references to Appendices
VIGNACOORT	12 9/16	8:30a	Instructions were given to Signal Squadron & representatives of signal troops in working aeroplane ground shutters.	
LAHOUSSOYE		2pm	Office at VIGNACOURT closed at 2 p.m. Reopened same hour at LA HOUSSOYE A pair to DAR was given to us the ran lines LPE with an exchange by which we got PC & RHA. Circuit diagram App. VI is attached	App VI
LAHOUSSOYE	13 9/16		No move. A pack W/T set joined us from ZCO under Sgt. Boreland comprised of 10 NCOs & men & 12 horses. A limbered G.S. wagon joined from VC for aeroplane petrol etc. The horses were in a very bad state. 5 horses joined for use of R.F.C. viz. 2 pack. 2 riders. 1 charger. No saddlery came so on morning of 15th pack horses complete were obtained from 21st C. Bde.	
LAHOUSSOYE	14 9/16		Divl. Hqrs did not move. The 3rd & 5th Cav Bdes & D. Bty RHA moved to a mill N of BRAY. on to L30 b.5 which was intended for our next Div2 Hqrs. Lt Brand went with ZRC & opened a distributing station for these units. Here he got into communication	

Instructions regarding War Diaries and Intelligence Summaries are contained in F. S. Regs., Part II. and the Staff Manual respectively. Title Pages will be prepared in manuscript.

WAR DIARY
or
INTELLIGENCE SUMMARY
(Erase heading not required.)

Army Form C. 2118.

Place	Date	Hour	Summary of Events and Information	Remarks and references to Appendices
	14 9/16		He also arranged with PCO to run an extension from ~~Fri~~ FRICOURT exchange to ROSE COTTAGE where G.O.C intended to wait during the attack. Direct extensions were also arranged by him from 41st & New Zealand Divs exchanges for use of our liaison officers.	
L3D6.5	15 9/16.	7am.	Divl Hqrs closed LAHOUSSOYE 7am. & reopened same hour at L3D6.5	
			Lt Bland & 2 MCs went at ROSE COTTAGE at same hour to be with G.O.C.	
			Visual was established to PC. & later to PE	
			PD & CRHA moved to near DERNANCOURT.	
			Circuits at 7am. are shown in App. VII.	
			Q who had arranged to stay at LAHOUSSOYE suddenly moved to L3D6.5 so their telephone to LAHOUSSOYE was taken away.	App. VII
"	16 9/16.		Same arrangements as for 15 9/16.	
			"B" Echelon informed they could use telephone X of 10am at BONNAY & DR ran to ~~them~~ from ZCO.	
"	17 9/16		Same arrangements as for 15 9/16. Rose Cottage office was not reopened.	
	18 9/16		Cable was laid to PC & PE.	
			Duty Sqdn found by this Divn at F15C6.4. ZRC telephone to 1st Fd. Sqdn was used by it.	

WAR DIARY
or
INTELLIGENCE SUMMARY
(Erase heading not required.)

Army Form C. 2118.

Instructions regarding War Diaries and Intelligence Summaries are contained in F. S. Regs., Part II. and the Staff Manual respectively. Title Pages will be prepared in manuscript.

Place	Date	Hour	Summary of Events and Information	Remarks and references to Appendices
L 3 D 6.5	19 9/16		RFC. W/T erected for taking press.	
	20 9/16		Same as for 19 9/16	
	21 9/16		Same as for 20 9/16.	
	22 9/16		Scheme with aeroplanes. 1st Report centre F 29 a 7.3. 2nd " " L 3 D 6.5.	
	23 9/16		No change.	
	24 9/16		Squadron signalling scheme.	
	25 9/16		No change.	
	26 9/16		Duty Sqdns formed by this Divn at F 15 c 6.4 & Rose Cottage. Comd of them was under ZRC. We sent 4 pigeons & 1 pigeoneer to each.	
	27 9/16		Telephones for Duty Sqdn found by us. Also pigeons.	
	28 9/16		~~The~~ Office at L 3 D 6.5 closed 12 noon. Reopened same time at F 24 c 6.4. We took over old ZRC office & cctn. Old ZRC – Y13 lines put through to PC & PE	

2449 Wt. W14957/M90 750,000 1/16 J.B.C. & A. Forms/C.2118/12.

Instructions regarding War Diaries and Intelligence Summaries are contained in F. S. Regs., Part II. and the Staff Manual respectively. Title Pages will be prepared in manuscript.

WAR DIARY
or
INTELLIGENCE SUMMARY
(Erase heading not required.)

Army Form C. 2118.

2nd SIGNAL SQUADRON No. Date. 2nd CAVALRY DIVISION

Place	Date	Hour	Summary of Events and Information	Remarks and references to Appendices
F24c64	29		PD came in circuit via OCO.	
			Circuits shown in App. VIII	App VIII
"	30th.		CRHA laid pair to PD & came on his exchange.	

Wiggle Capt
Comdg 2nd Sig. Sqdn

2449 Wt. W14957/M90 750,000 1/16 J.B.C. & A. Forms/C.2118/12.

Appendix I

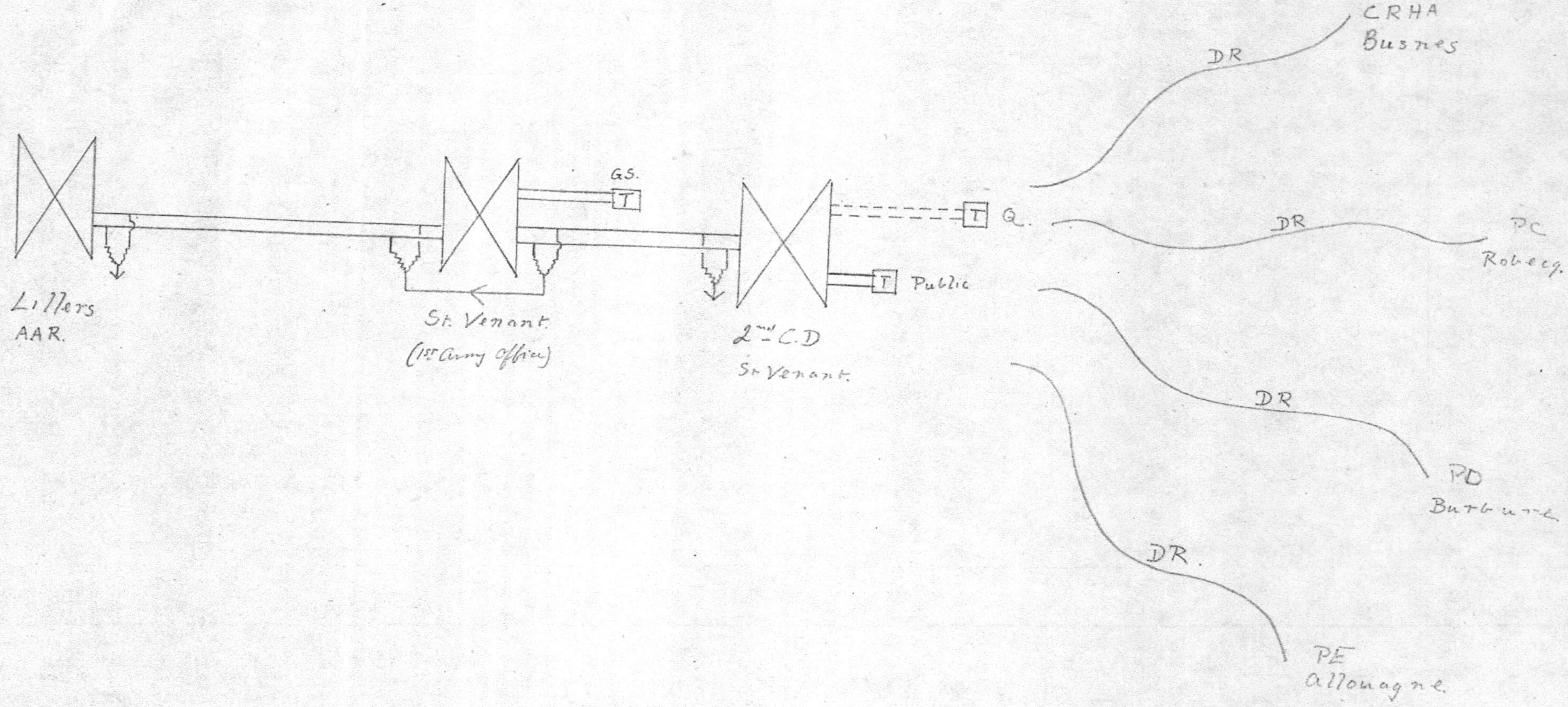

Lillers
AAR.
G.S.
T
St. Venant.
(1st Army Office)
T
Q.
T
Public
2nd C.D
St Venant.
DR
CRHA
Busnes
DR
PC
Robecq.
DR
PD
Burbure
DR.
PE
allouagne.

2nd C.D.

Cct DIAGRAM

/9/16

Appendix Z.

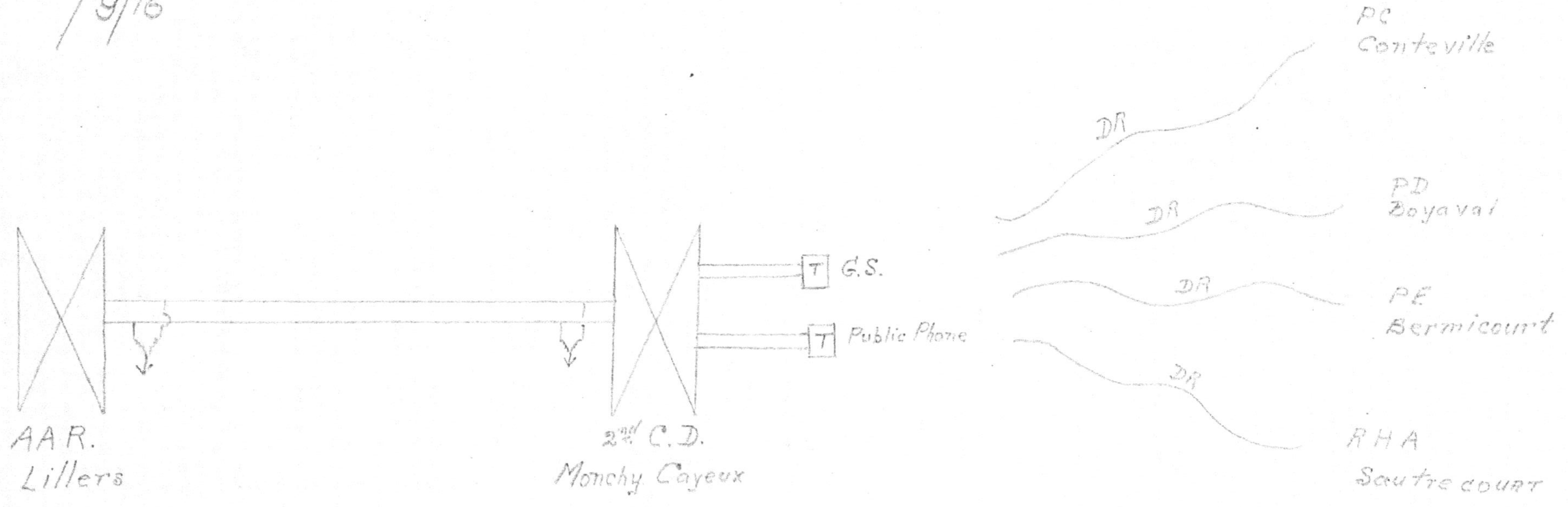

Appendix 3.

2nd C.D.
Cct Diagram
/9/16

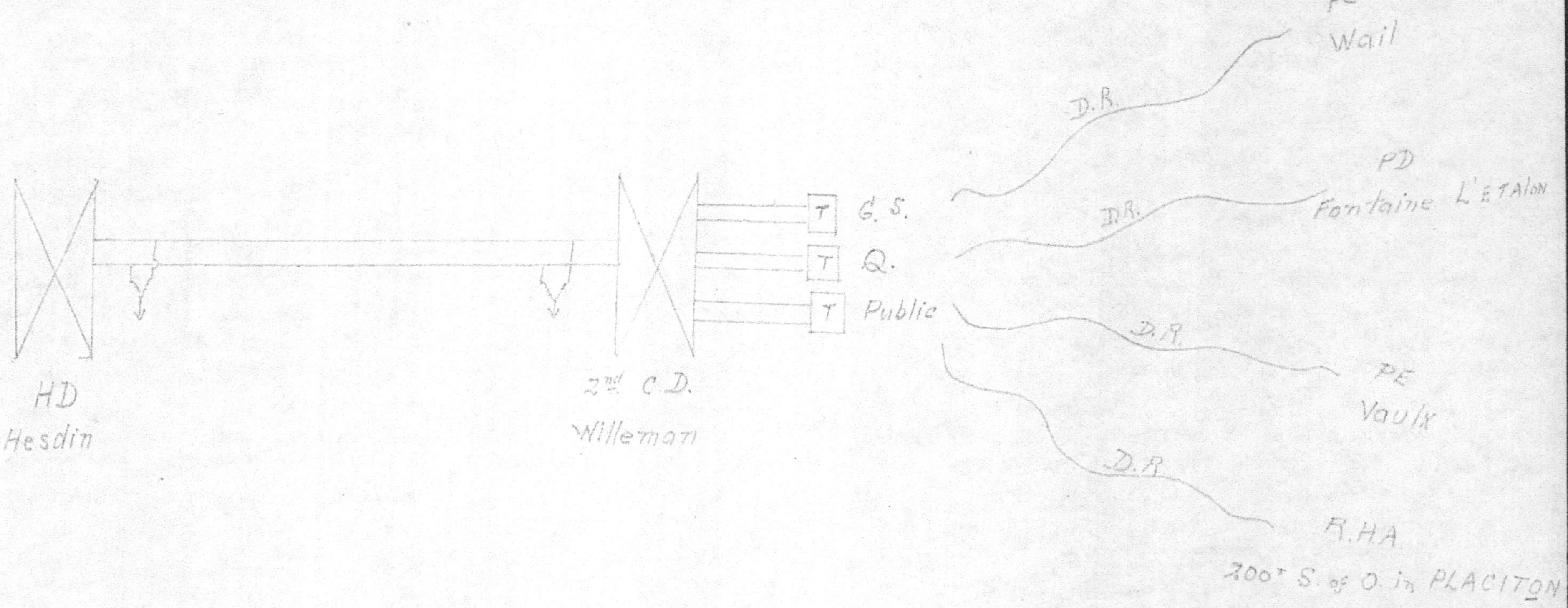

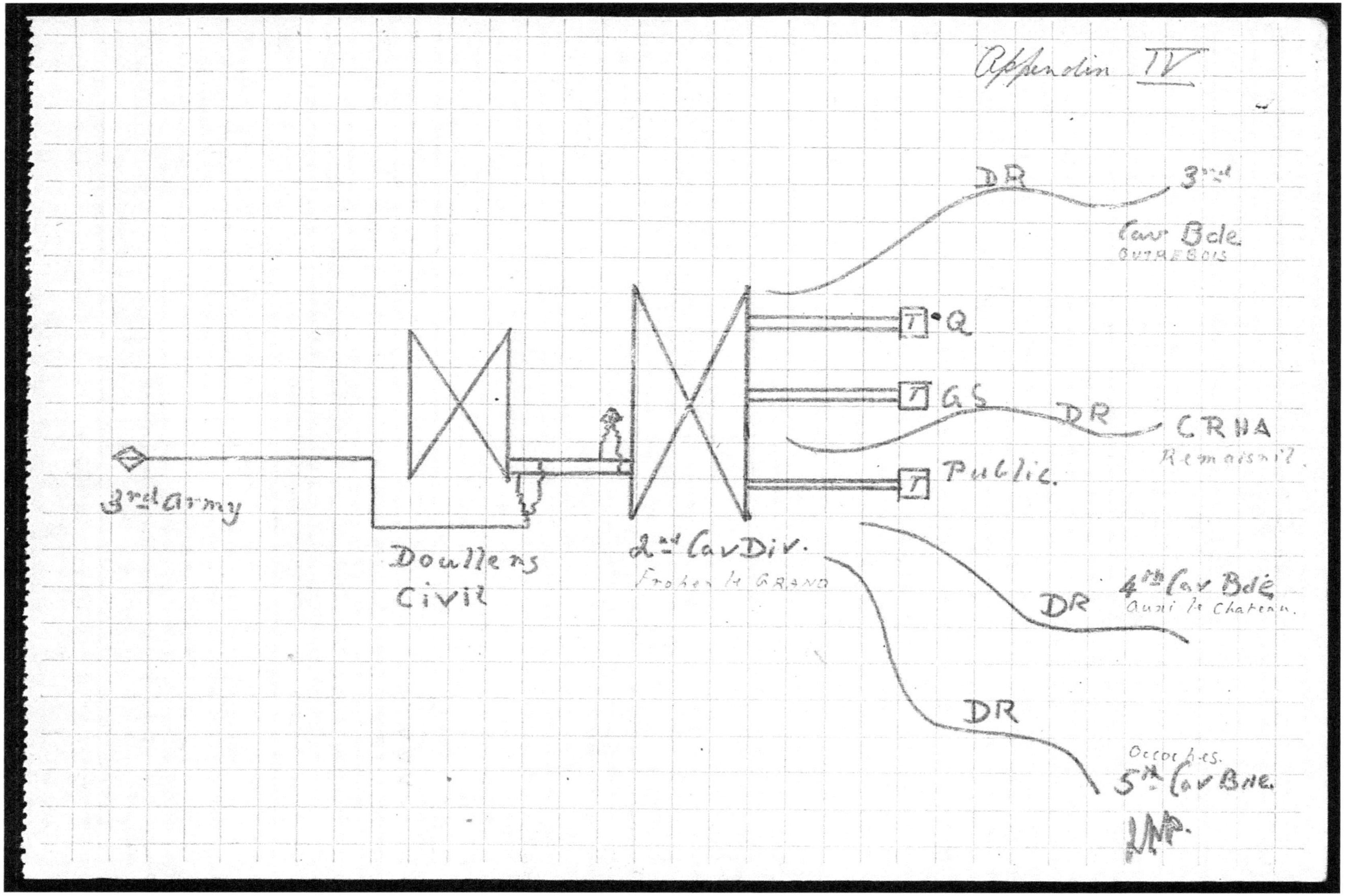

Appendix IV
3rd Army
Doullens Civil
2nd Cav Div.
Frohen le Grand
DR
3rd Cav Bde
Outrebois
Q
GS
DR
CRHA
Remaisnil
Public
DR
4th Cav Bde
Auxi le Chateau
DR
Occoches
5th Cav Bde

Appendix V

2nd CAVALRY DIVISION

Circuits /9/16

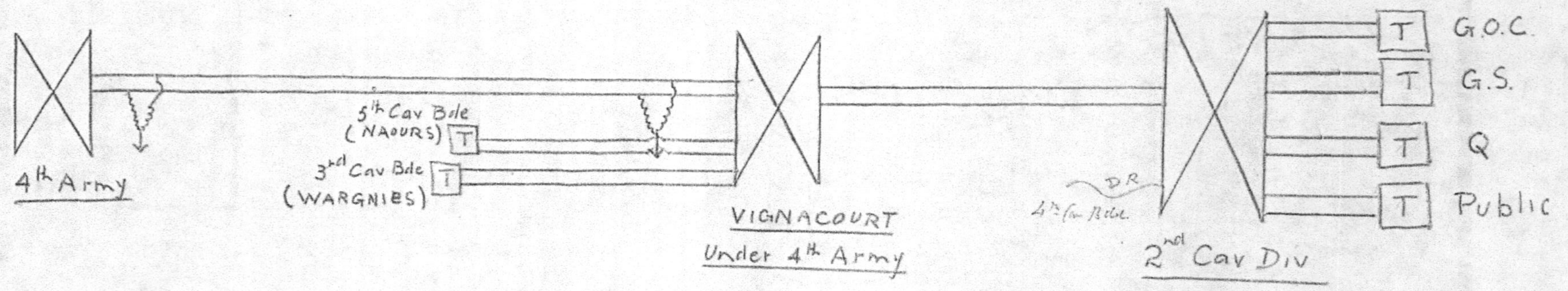

2nd C.D.
Cct Diagram
/9/16

Appendix G.

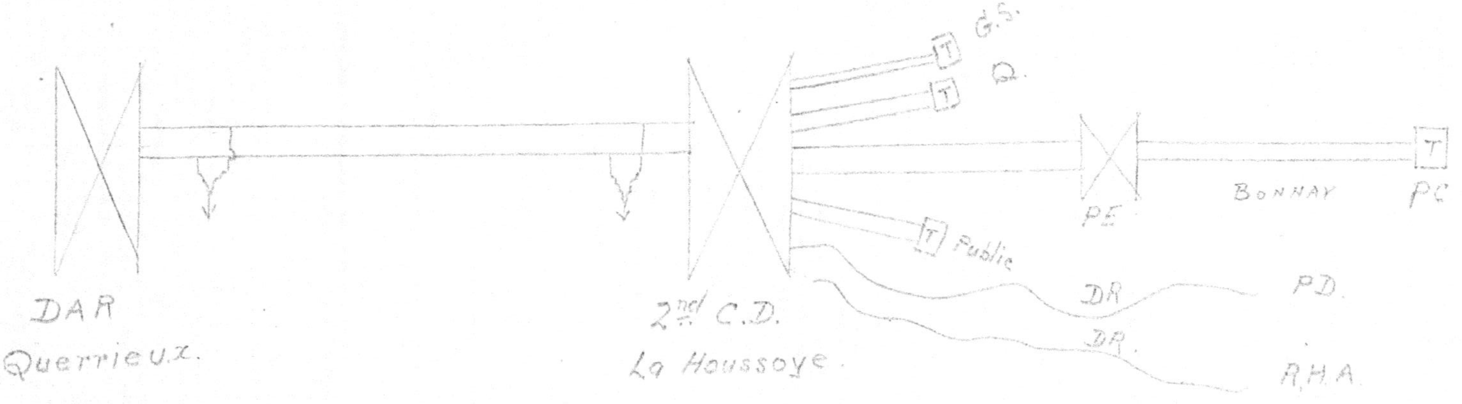

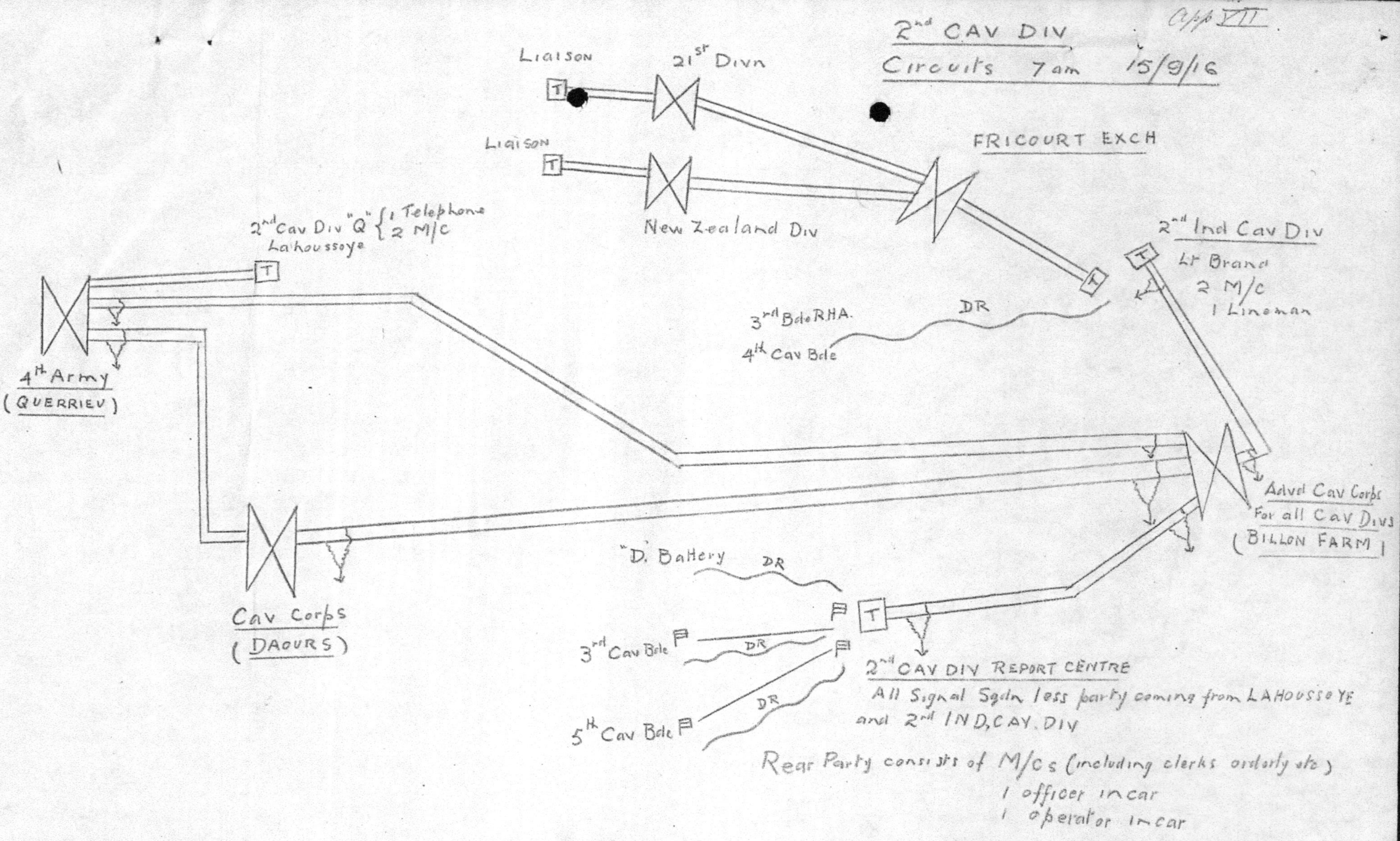
App VII
2nd CAV DIV
Circuits 7 am 15/9/16
FRICOURT EXCH
Liaison
21st Divn
Liaison
New Zealand Div
2nd Ind Cav Div
Lt Brand
2 M/C
1 Lineman
2nd Cav Div "Q" Lahoussoye { 1 Telephone 2 M/C
4th Army (QUERRIEU)
3rd Bde RHA.
4th Cav Bde
DR
Advd Cav Corps For all Cav Divs (BILLON FARM)
Cav Corps (DAOURS)
"D" Battery
DR
3rd Cav Bde
DR
5th Cav Bde
DR
2nd CAV DIV REPORT CENTRE
All Signal Sqdn less party coming from LAHOUSSOYE and 2nd IND, CAV. DIV
Rear Party consists of M/Cs (including clerks orderly etc)
1 officer in car
1 operator in car

2nd CAV DIVN CCTS

App VIII

Exclusive of forward lines and DRs

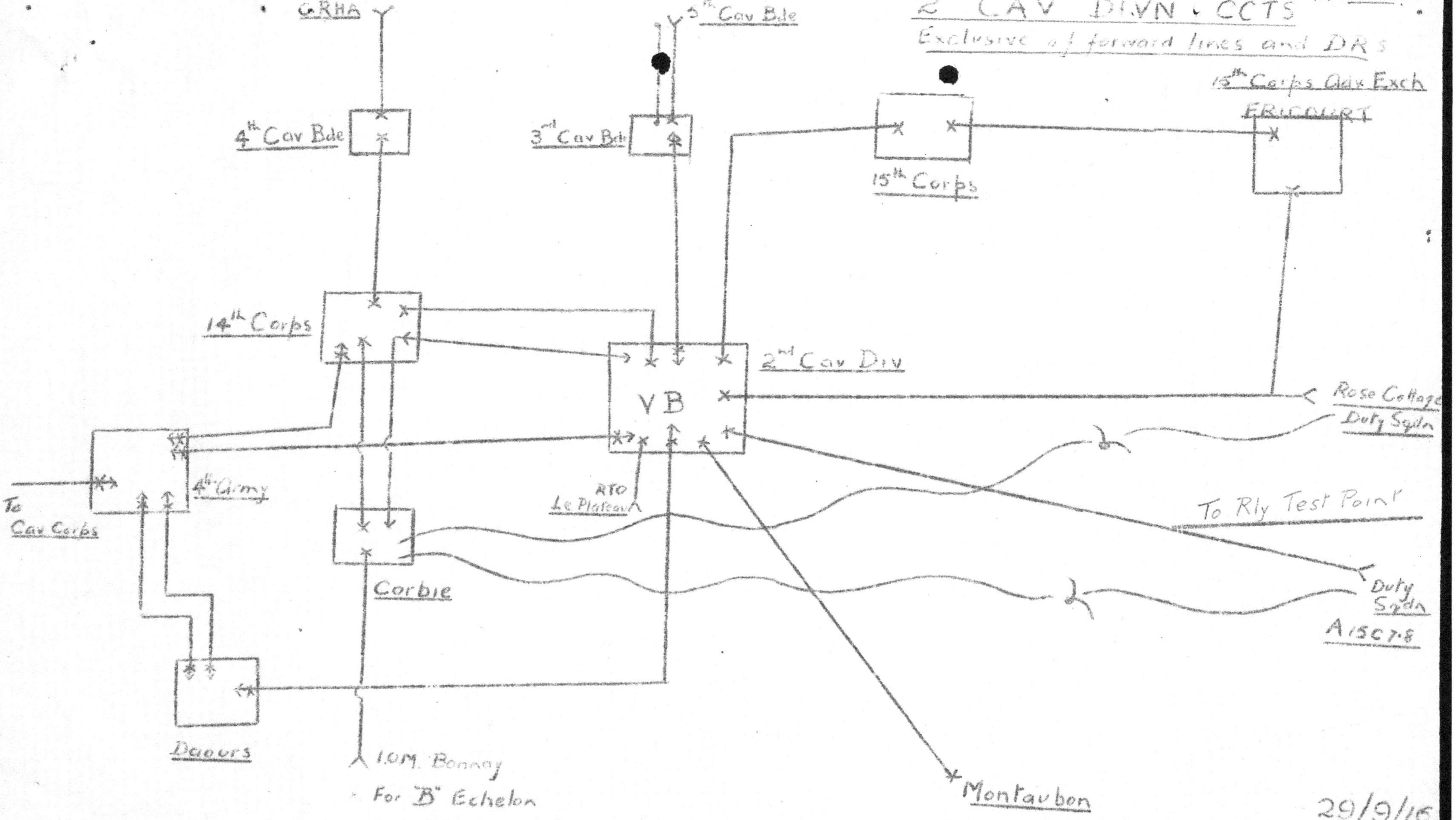

29/9/16

SECRET.

Vol 15

WAR DIARY

of

2nd SIGNAL SQUADRON, R.E.

OCTOBER, 1916.

VOL. ~~XXVI~~.

Instructions regarding War Diaries and Intelligence Summaries are contained in F. S. Regs., Part II. and the Staff Manual respectively. Title Pages will be prepared in manuscript.

WAR DIARY
or
~~INTELLIGENCE SUMMARY~~
(Erase heading not required.)

Army Form C. 2118.

Place	Date	Hour	Summary of Events and Information	Remarks and references to Appendices
F24C6.4. (Albertshut)	1 10/16	8pm	Positions of Brigades ~~at~~ for 10am the following day notified.	
"	2 10/16		Brigades moved to new bivouacs. A pair of lines built to each & put on P.D. exchange. Lines to P.C. superimposed on & P.D. became intermediate. For circuits mentioned see App I. DADOS moved to BURE also did the Amm. Park.	App I
"	3 10/16		Pair of lines laid to the supply Column who had moved to within 800 yds of P.D.	
"	4 10/16		~~Lt~~ Lt Paton (6 DGs) & 2 men per brigade joined the unit for work under the Cavalry Corps who were clearing the area. We contributed 2 men making a total of 10. Last day the Div found a duty again. See therefore recalled our telephones. Sent out no more pigeons	
"	5 10/16		Party of 10 men found by the Division commenced work for the Cavalry Corps. New docket system introduced from ZCO.	
"	6 10/16		Nothing to report.	

Instructions regarding War Diaries and Intelligence Summaries are contained in F. S. Regs., Part II. and the Staff Manual respectively. Title Pages will be prepared in manuscript.

WAR DIARY
or
~~INTELLIGENCE~~ SUMMARY
(Erase heading not required.)

Army Form C. 2118.

Place	Date	Hour	Summary of Events and Information	Remarks and references to Appendices
F24C64	7 10/16		Pigeons given to Brigades to practice handling them & to use ~~with~~ on their schemes. The W/T set went to DAOURS for schemes arranged by Cavalry Corps.	
"	8 10/16		Pigeons given to Bdes for schemes	
"	9 10/16		Same as 8 10/16	
"	10th		8 RHA go into action. The lines ½ to 2nd Ind. Dismounted party were extended to the wagon lines & a pair was laid from Bde Hqrs to LONGUEVAL Test Point. They were joined to the 21st DA exchange under whose orders they came. The 21st DA had direct communication to FRICOURT Exch. DRs went to the wagon lines from YB. Pigeons as before.	
11th	11th		Cavalry Corps made made switches in lines with a view to opening a report centre at ALBERT. Our ccts then became as shown in app II. Pigeons as before. Visit paid to Sigs 12th Div in case a gap was made & the advance through their area. A pair built for 2nd Ind Cav. Sqdn to FRICOURT Exch. as their former pair were picked up by someone unknown	App II

Instructions regarding War Diaries and Intelligence Summaries are contained in F. S. Regs., Part II. and the Staff Manual respectively. Title Pages will be prepared in manuscript.

WAR DIARY
or
~~INTELLIGENCE SUMMARY~~
(Erase heading not required.)

Army Form C. 2118.

3rd Signal Squadron RE

Place	Date	Hour	Summary of Events and Information	Remarks and references to Appendices
F26C64	12th		Two terminal boards were removed by Sigs ZCO	
〃	13th		Ten line exchange installed vice 30 line board.	
			Pack W/T returned from DAOURS	
〃	14th		B Pack W/T rejoined Wireless Cav Corps at ALBERT.	
〃	15th		Nothing to report.	
〃	16th		Lt. Drake assumed command of the Sqdn at 6pm	
〃	17th to		Nothing to report.	
〃	27th		Usual routine	
〃	28th		3rd Bde. RHA came out of the line and went into bivouac at 4 PM at Point E.22.d. (Albert combined) Telephone communication opened with them through 4th Cav. Bde. Signals at 6.45 PM	

2449 Wt. W14957/M90 750,000 1/16 J.B.C. & A. Forms/C.2118/12.

Army Form C. 2118.

Instructions regarding War Diaries and Intelligence Summaries are contained in F. S. Regs., Part II. and the Staff Manual respectively. Title Pages will be prepared in manuscript.

WAR DIARY
or
~~INTELLIGENCE SUMMARY~~

(Erase heading not required.)

2d Signal Squadron R.E.

Place	Date	Hour	Summary of Events and Information	Remarks and references to Appendices
F.24.c.6.4	29th		Nothing to report, usual routine	
	30th		Usual routine	
	31st.		Nothing to report.	

[illegible]

Lieut 11th Hussars

Cmdg 2d Signal Squadron R.E.

2449 Wt. W14957/M90 750,000 1/16 J.B.C. & A. Forms/C.2118/12.

App I

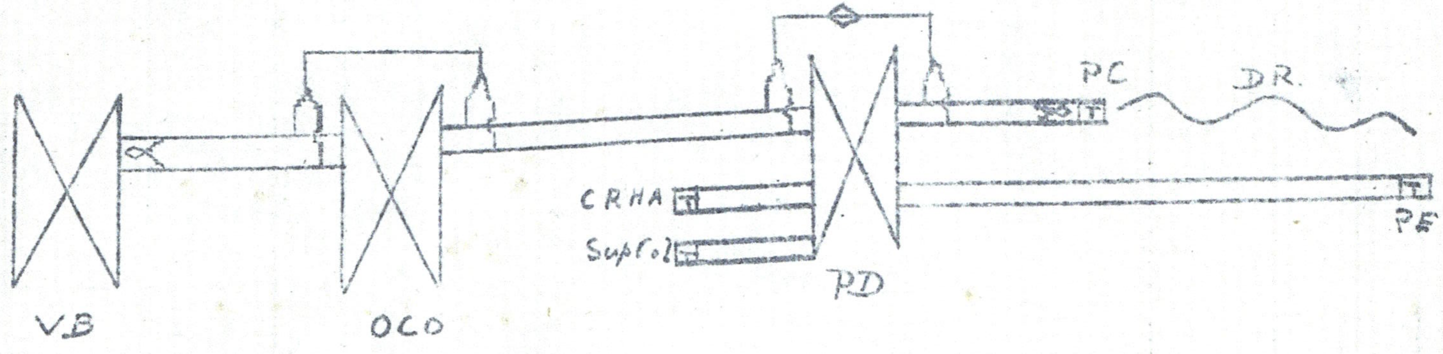

Additional cells

2.10.16

App II.

2nd Cav Div Circuits

11.10.16

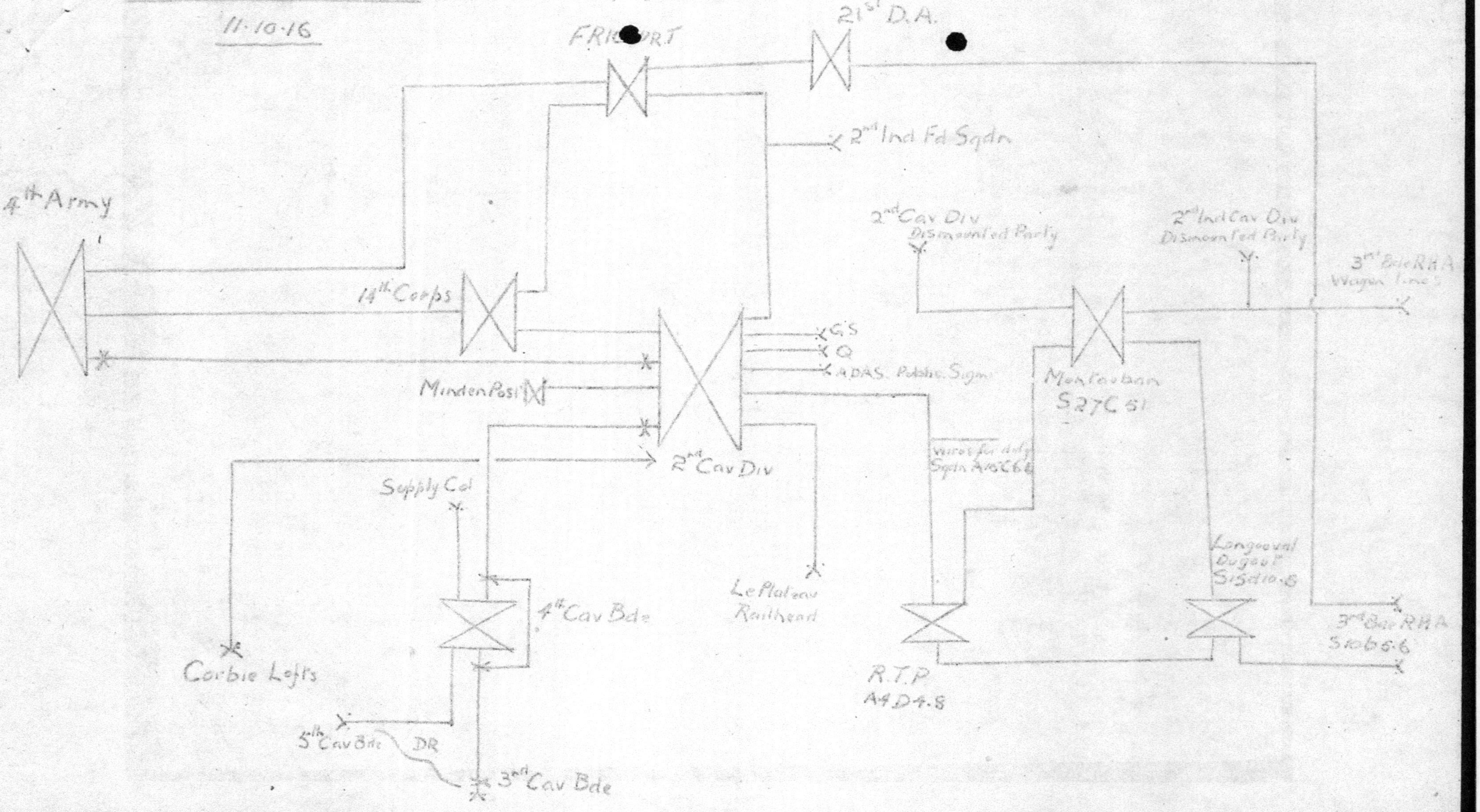

SECRET.

Vol 16

W A R   D I A R Y

of

2nd SIGNAL SQUADRON, R.E.

NOVEMBER, 1916.

VOL. XXVII.

Army Form C. 2118.

Instructions regarding War Diaries and Intelligence Summaries are contained in F. S. Regs., Part II. and the Staff Manual respectively. Title Pages will be prepared in manuscript.

WAR DIARY

~~or~~

~~INTELLIGENCE SUMMARY~~

(Erase heading not required.)

2d Signal Squadron R.E.

Place	Date	Hour	Summary of Events and Information	Remarks and references to Appendices
F24.C.6.4	1/11/16		Nothing to report, usual routine	
	2nd.	10AM	Mounted party including mounted personnel of R.F.C. attached proceeded to new bivouac near MEAULTE	
E28.b.9.9	3rd.	10AM	Office closed at F24.C.6.4 and re-opened at same hour at new camp. D.A.R. and the 3 Brigades were on by Morse and telephone at that hour 4th Cav. Bde. intermediate to 3rd Bde. who transmit for 5th Cav. Bde. Z.R.C. intermediate on D.A.R. circuit 2/Lieut Levander 3rd Hussars rejoined his Regiment to day	Appx 1
	4th "		Settling in, patrolling new lines etc.	
	5th "		Pair of lines run out from V.B. to PD bringing PE direct on to Divl. exchange Morse and telephone	appx 2
	6th "		Nothing to report	
	7th "		Usual routine	

2449 Wt. W14957/M90 750,000 1/16 J.B.C. & A. Forms/C.2118/12.

Army Form C. 2118.

WAR DIARY
or
~~INTELLIGENCE SUMMARY~~
(Erase heading not required.)

Instructions regarding War Diaries and Intelligence Summaries are contained in F. S. Regs., Part II. and the Staff Manual respectively. Title Pages will be prepared in manuscript.

2nd Signal Squadron R.E.

Place	Date	Hour	Summary of Events and Information	Remarks and references to Appendices
	8/11/16	7 AM.	Squadron marched for new billets at BELLOY sur somme.	
		12 NOON	Office closed at E.28.b.9.9. and reopened at BELLOY same hour communication to 4th Army direct by morse and telephone, to PD at BUSSY-LES-DAOURS (~~DOUARS~~) at 3.10 pm. to PE at ALLONVILLE at 3.30 pm. and to PC by orderly from DAOURS (~~DOUARS~~) signal office all by telephone Local offices G.S, + Q. and G.O.C. at Chateau Capt. James with R.F.C. personnel left.	Appx. 3
	9th "		Divl. Head Qrs and Signals remain in billets. PC + PD Offices closed at 7 AM. PE at 7.30 AM. P.D. reopened at BELLOY school at 2.5 PM no communication to PC + PE except by orderly. PC are at BILLET-BOURDON. PE at YZEUX chateau	Appx. 4
	10th "	7 AM.	Squadron marched for BUIGNY ST MACLOU	
		10 AM.	Office closed at BELLOY	
		12 NOON	Office should have opened at BUIGNY but owing to a fault on the existing Z.C.O. line did not open till 1.35 PM. communication with Z.C.O. direct only communication to Brigades is by orderly PC at LE-TITRE, PD at CHATEAU BOIS DE LE L'ABBEY, PE at NEUILLY L'HOPITAL	Appx 5
	11th "	7 AM.	Squadron marched for LIGESCOURT. Office closed at BUIGNY at 10 AM and reopened LIGESCOURT same hour. Communication to Z.C.O. on superimposed pair, to PD by morse and telephone at 5.50 pm to PC and PE	

2449 Wt. W14957/M90 750,000 1/16 J.B.C. & A. Forms/C.2118/12.

Instructions regarding War Diaries and Intelligence Summaries are contained in F. S. Regs., Part II. and the Staff Manual respectively. Title Pages will be prepared in manuscript.

WAR DIARY
or
~~INTELLIGENCE SUMMARY~~
(Erase heading not required.)

Army Form C. 2118.

2d Signal Squadron RE

Place	Date	Hour	Summary of Events and Information	Remarks and references to Appendices
LIGESCOURT	11th		by telephone at 10pm + 20pm respectively Local circuits G S and Q at 10 AM	
	12th to 15th		Signal office construction, Inside wiring etc. Cable laid by O.C. RHA to V.B. office on 12th, Supply column put through by telephone on P.E. pair on 13th	
	16th	7 AM	Signal Office complete came into force test board and sets were placed in permanent positions. Cable laid by O.C. RHA taken up owing to his move from Chateau 1 mile S.W. of L in LIGESCOURT to Farm 1 mile NNE of CRECY. New line commenced to him at his new billet. Clipping horses for first time commenced to day.	
	17th			
	18th		Hd Qrs RHA. put through on telephone, line built on French system through at 10.15 AM line proved clear. Conference of Signal Squadron leaders at Cavalry Corps Signals	
	19th		Usual routine pair laid to new site of "Q" office. 24 line exchange installed at 11pm working O.K. at 12 MN.	
	20th		Usual routine	
	21st		Poling commenced to Divisional School at DOURIEZ	

Instructions regarding War Diaries and Intelligence Summaries are contained in F. S. Regs., Part II. and the Staff Manual respectively. Title Pages will be prepared in manuscript.

WAR DIARY
or
INTELLIGENCE SUMMARY
(Erase heading not required.)

Army Form C. 2118.

2d Signal Squadron R.E.

Place	Date	Hour	Summary of Events and Information	Remarks and references to Appendices
LIGESCOURT	22d		Lieut Brand completed line to Divisional school at DOURIEZ commenced poling to 2d Field Squadron at PONCHES ESTRUVAL	
	23d		Work on Field Squadron line. Lieut A.P. BODEN (M.C.) 12th Lancers joined from XIV Corps.	
	24th		Field Squadron line completed	
	25th		Usual routine	
	26th		Usual routine. G.O.C. 2d Cavalry Division inspected all Squadron billets	
	27th		usual routine. Flag drill in the morning	
	28th		nothing to report, usual routine with Flag drill	
	29th / 30th		usual routine. Signalling etc.	appx. 6

[signature]
Captain
XI Hussars
Cmdg. 2d Signal Sqdn

Appx I

2nd Cav Division

Cct Diagram 3/11/16

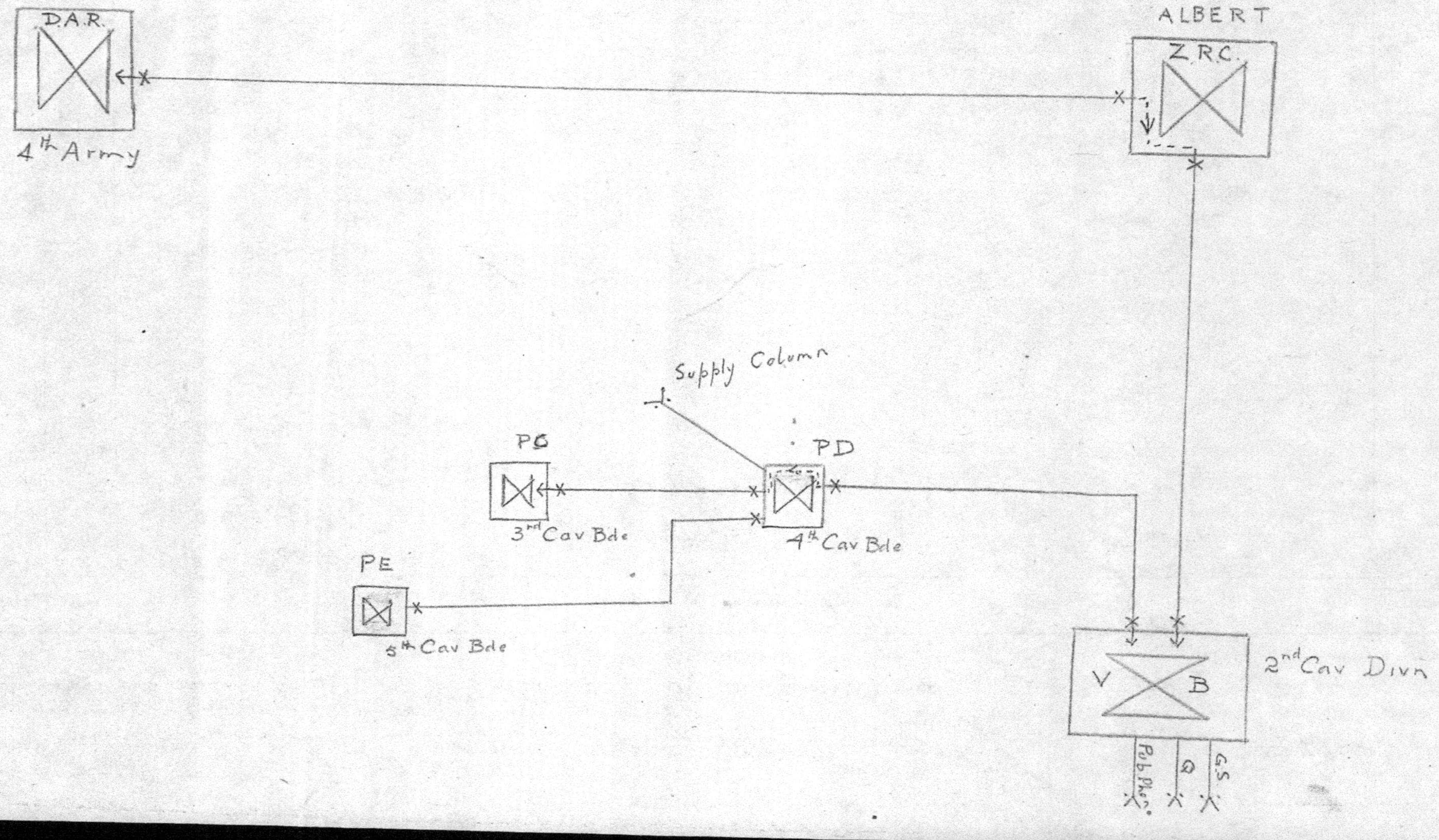

Appx 2

2nd Cav Divn

Cct Diagram 5/11/16

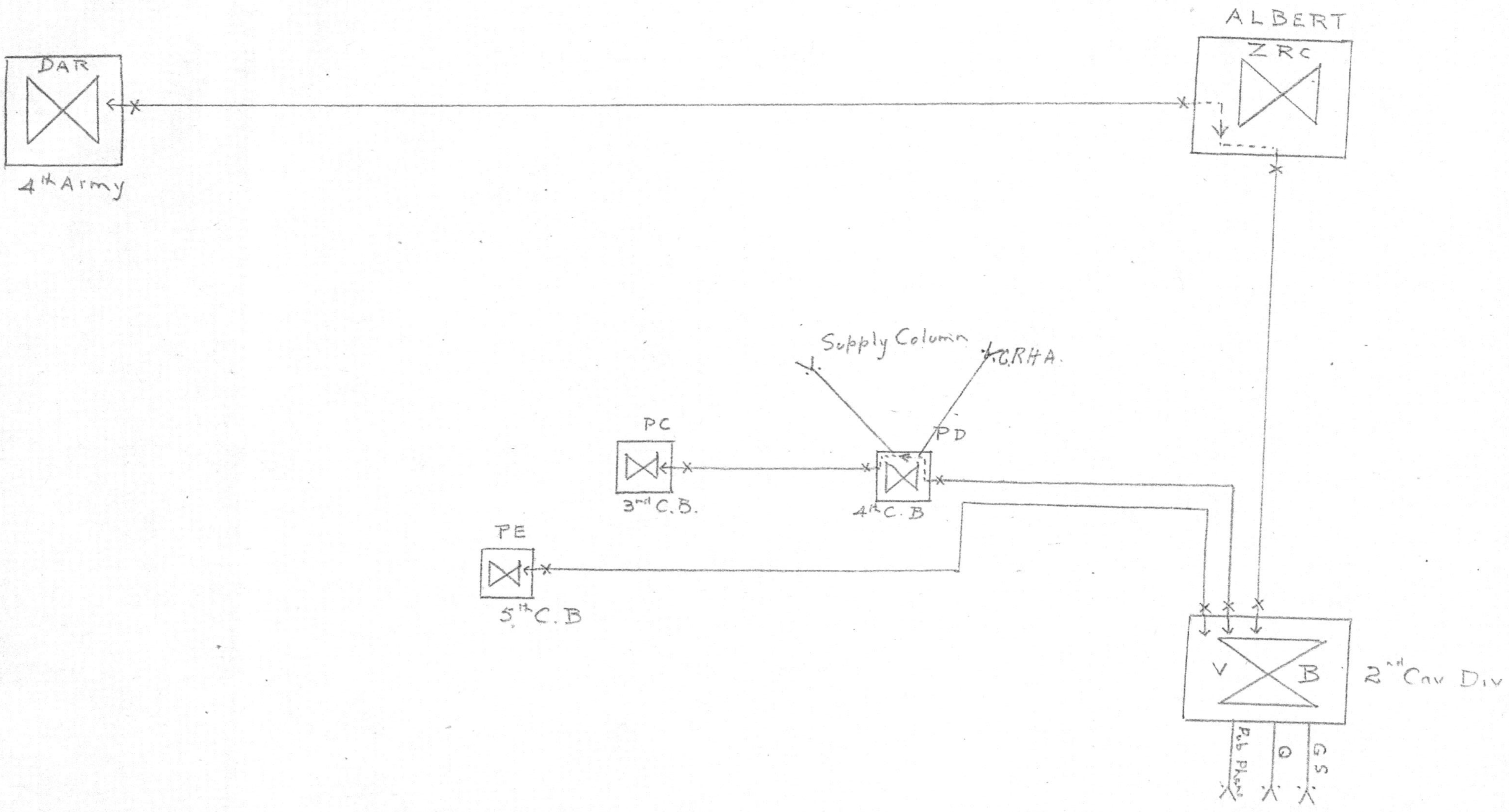

2nd CAV DIV

Circuit Diagram 8·11·16

Appx. 8.

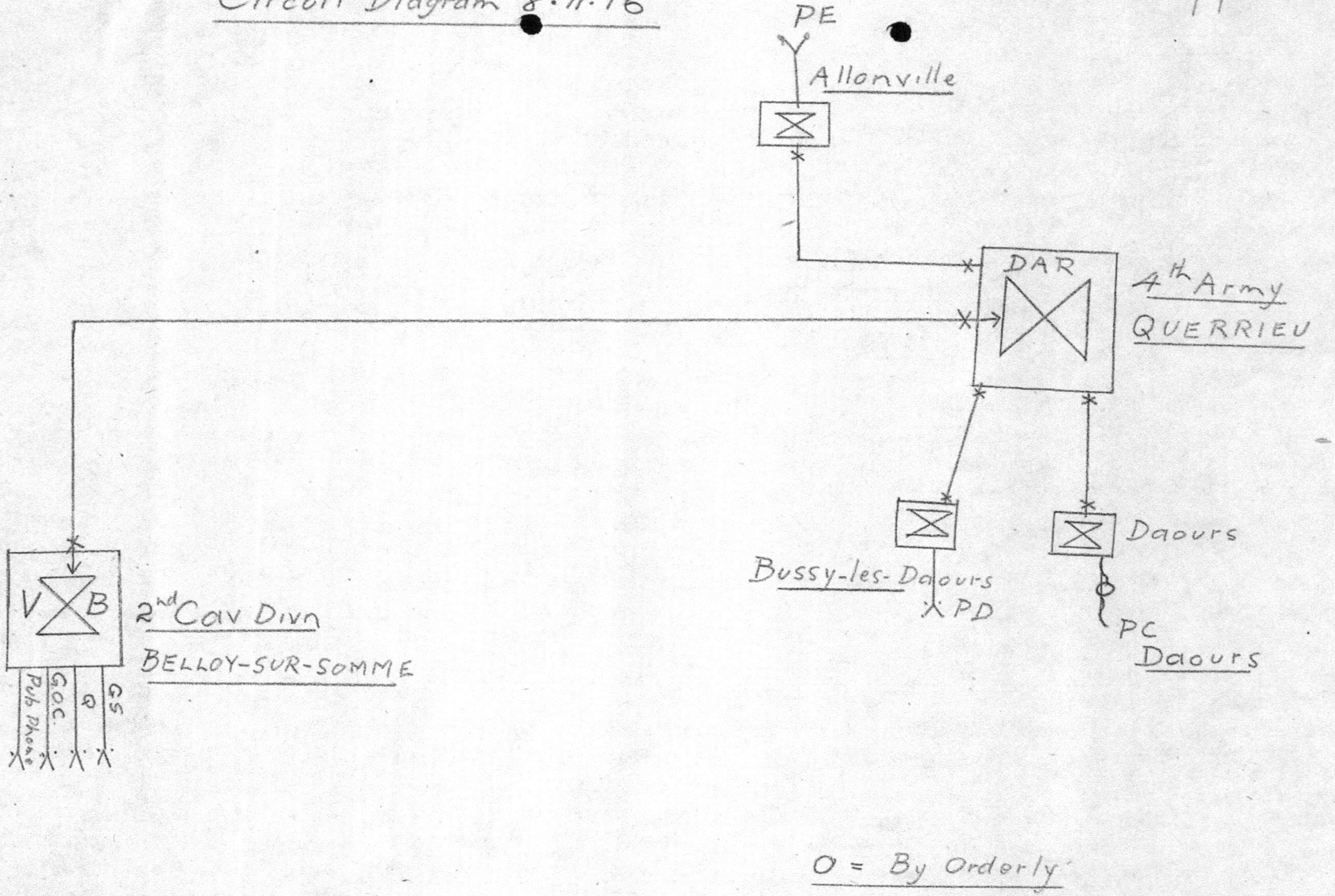

Appx 4

2nd Cav Div

Circuit Diagram 9/11/16

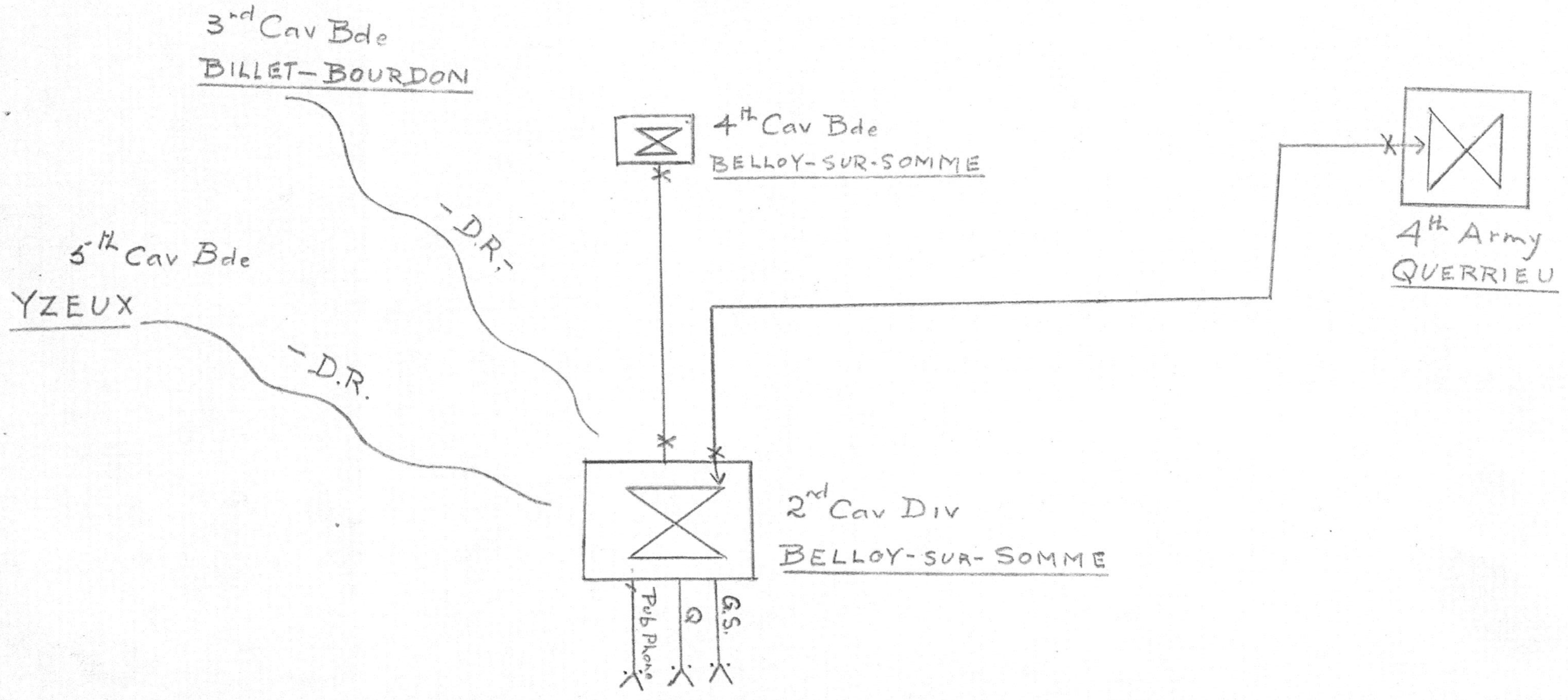

2nd Cav. Div.

Circuit Diagram 10/11/16

Appx. 5

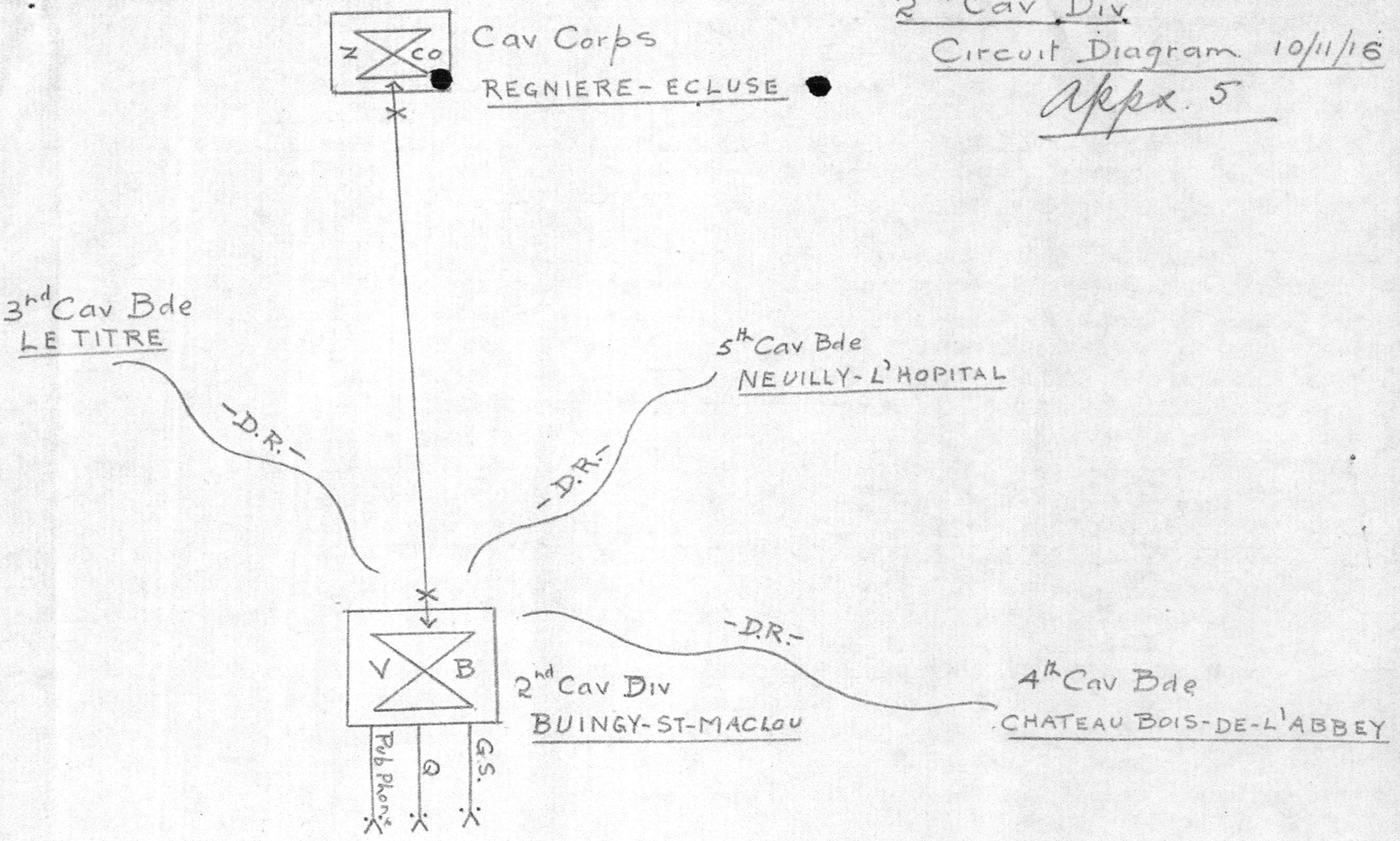

Appx 6

2nd Cavalry Division Circuit Diagram

31/11/16.

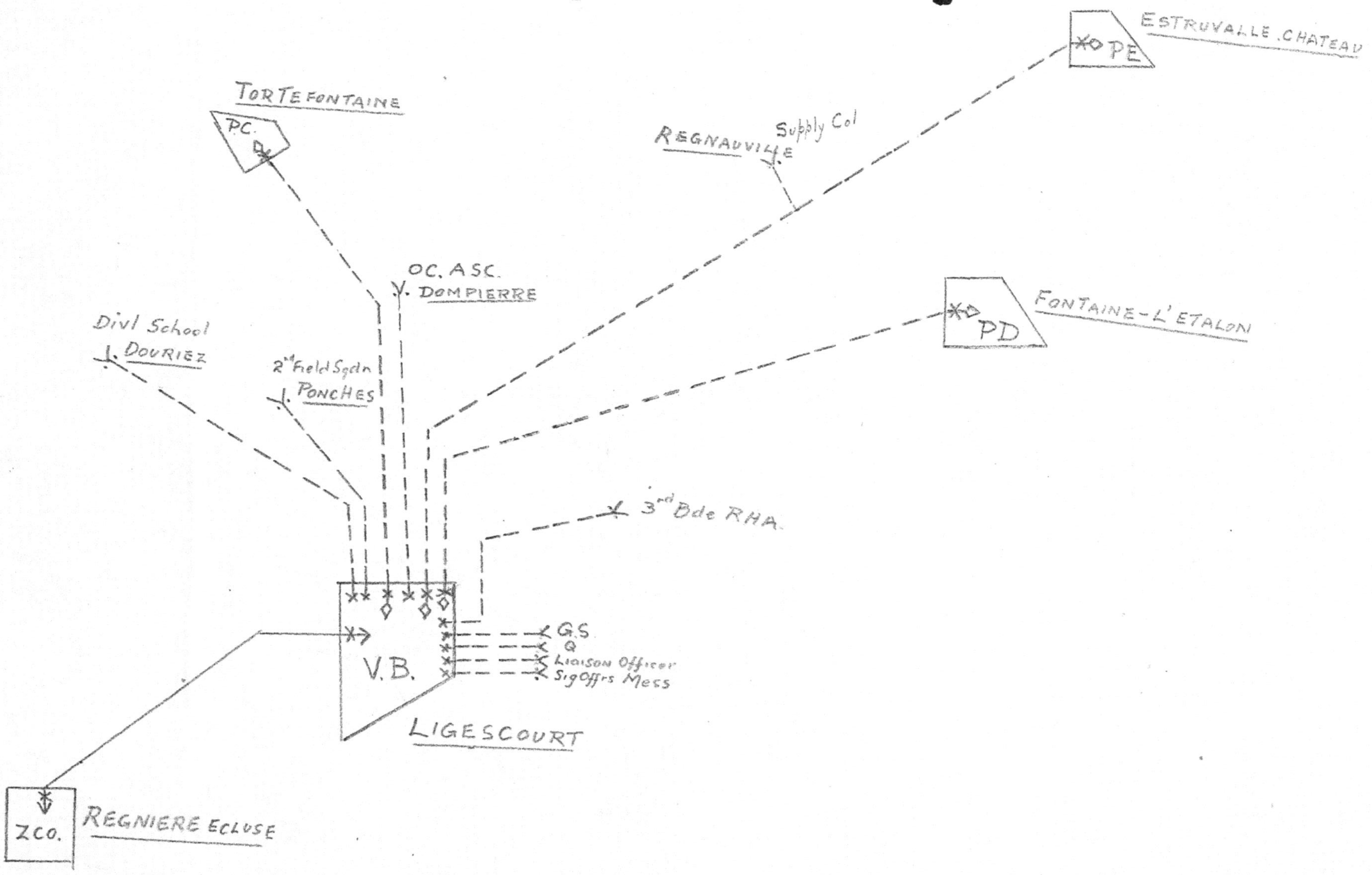

CONFIDENTIAL.

Vol 17

WAR DIARY

of

2nd SIGNAL SQUADRON, R.E.

DECEMBER, 1916.

VOL. XXVIII.

Instructions regarding War Diaries and Intelligence Summaries are contained in F. S. Regs., Part II. and the Staff Manual respectively. Title Pages will be prepared in manuscript.

WAR DIARY
or
~~INTELLIGENCE SUMMARY~~
(Erase heading not required.)

Army Form C. 2118.

2nd Signal Squadron R.E.

Place	Date	Hour	Summary of Events and Information	Remarks and references to Appendices
LIGESCOURT	1/12/16		Usual routine, Work on Divisional school line several poles had been Knocked down. Signalling 9.45 to 10.45 AM	FW
	2nd		Usual routine.	FW
	3d		Working party detailed to assist parties from Z. C.O. erecting new lines alongside existing ones running to PC. PD. PE.	FW
	4th "		Usual routine	FW
	5th "		Usual routine, working party still out with party from Z C.O on line construction.	FW
	6th "		Nothing to report	FW
	7th "		Usual routine, signalling etc.	FW
	8th "		Nothing to report	FW
	9th "		Routine as usual, Signalling, reading tests	FW
	10th "		Nothing to report	FW

Instructions regarding War Diaries and Intelligence Summaries are contained in F. S. Regs., Part II. and the Staff Manual respectively. Title Pages will be prepared in manuscript.

WAR DIARY
or
~~INTELLIGENCE SUMMARY~~
(Erase heading not required.)

Army Form C. 2118.

2nd Signal Squadron R.E.

Place	Date	Hour	Summary of Events and Information	Remarks and references to Appendices
LIGESCOURT	11/12/18		Usual routine, signalling station work	FW
	12th "		Nothing to report	FW
	13th		Usual routine signalling, station work	
	14th		Same as 13th "	
	15th		Nothing to report	
	16th		Visual scheme, new line laid to Hd-qrs R.H.A. airline replaced by cable.	FW
	17th		Usual Routine. Old "Q" line and Liaison officers line picked up, Liaison officers line replaced with cable	
	18th		Nothing to Report	
	19th		First Visual signalling scheme between Signal Troops of the division and the Signal Squadron, Stationary ~~scheme~~ lasting from 10 Am until 12.30 Pm.	FW FW
	20th		Usual Routine.	FW
	21st		A.D.A.S. Cavalry Corps inspected the Signal Office, Billets, Horses and the Squadron. Buzzer reading classes started.	FW
	22nd		Mounted Signallers started instruction in line maintainance jointing and repairing airline. Buzzer reading in the evening otherwise usual routine.	FW

2449 Wt. W14957/M90 750,000 1/16 J.B.C. & A. Forms/C.2118/12.

Army Form C. 2118.

Instructions regarding War Diaries and Intelligence Summaries are contained in F. S. Regs., Part II. and the Staff Manual respectively. Title Pages will be prepared in manuscript.

WAR DIARY
~~or~~
~~INTELLIGENCE SUMMARY~~

(Erase heading not required.)

2nd Signal Squadron R.E.

Place	Date	Hour	Summary of Events and Information	Remarks and references to Appendices
LIBESCOURT	23rd		Very heavy storm most of the day causing several trees to fall down on the lines, all lines were temporarily put through with cable	WB
	24th		All lines were properly repaired and working O.K., G.O.C. inspected competition in the Squadron for the best mounted man in drill order (Pte Higgins Royal Scots Greys.) Best cyclist in marching order (Spr Cooper R.E.) Best driver with pair of horses (Dvr Davies R.E.)	WB
	25th		Christmas Day.	WB
	26th		Usual Routine.	WB
	27th		All cable on local circuits replaced by airline except Liaison Officers line. R.H.A. line started.	WB
	28th		R.H.A. line finished. Usual Routine. A.D.M.S. put on the Telephone.	WB

Army Form C. 2118.

Instructions regarding War Diaries and Intelligence Summaries are contained in F. S. Regs., Part II. and the Staff Manual respectively. Title Pages will be prepared in manuscript.

WAR DIARY
~~or~~
~~INTELLIGENCE~~ SUMMARY
(Erase heading not required.)

2nd Signal Squadron R.E.

Place	Date	Hour	Summary of Events and Information	Remarks and references to Appendices
LIGESCOURT	29th		Airline to the Orderly Room and Liaison officer run. One pair run and joined to LIGESCOURT – CRECY French civil. Otherwise usual Routine.	FW
	30th		French civil LIGESCOURT — CRECY — ESTRÉES – LES – CRECY run through and lead in to 4th Machine Gun Squadron office at ESTRÉE-LES-CRECY line through. ~~at~~ and on divisional exchange 2·10 P.M. New trunk started to ESTRÊE-LES-CRECY for 4th and 5th Brigades.	FW
	31st		New trunk for 4th and 5th Brigades finished between ESTRÊE-LES-CRECY road and WADICOURT. 4th Bde put through on new route working O.K. Signalling course class arrived in Billets.	FW
	~~Jan 1st 1914~~		~~Work continued on the 5th Bde line.~~	~~FW~~
	~~2nd~~		~~Same as yesterday Signal course assisted~~	~~FW~~

F.W. Drake Captain
R.E.
Commanding 2nd Signal Squadron

2449 Wt. W14957/M90 750,000 1/16 J.B.C. & A. Forms/C.2118/12.

CONFIDENTIAL.

Vol 18

WAR DIARY

of

2nd SIGNAL SQUADRON, R.E.

JANUARY, ~~1916.~~ 1917

VOL. XXIX.

Army Form C. 2118.

WAR DIARY
or
INTELLIGENCE SUMMARY
(Erase heading not required.)

Instructions regarding War Diaries and Intelligence Summaries are contained in F. S. Regs., Part II. and the Staff Manual respectively. Title Pages will be prepared in manuscript.

2nd Signal Sqdn R.E.

Place	Date	Hour	Summary of Events and Information	Remarks and references to Appendices
LIGESCOURT	Jan 1st	1917	Work continued on 5th Bde line.	FW
	2nd		Same as yesterday Signal course assisted.	FW
	3rd		5th Bde line through and working O.K. 2 PM. Trunk to LE-BOISLE now completed and working. New trunk to DOMPIERRE started.	FW
	4th		Usual Routine.	FW
	5th		DOMPIERRE trunk continued but not finished. Otherwise usual routine	FW
	6th		Work continued on DOMPIERRE trunk.	FW
	7th		Line started from 4th Bde Signal Office to the supply column via CHERIENNE. OC ASC put on DOMPIERRE trunk with T off to A.D.M.S.	FW
	8th		Work on supply column continued. ~~met~~ A.D Signals and O.C. 2nd Signal Squadron inspected 3rd Signal Troop and the three Regiments in the 3rd Cav Bde.	FW

2449 Wt. W14957/M90 750,000 1/16 J.B.C. & A. Forms/C.2118/12.

Instructions regarding War Diaries and Intelligence Summaries are contained in F. S. Regs., Part II. and the Staff Manual respectively. Title Pages will be prepared in manuscript.

WAR DIARY
or
~~INTELLIGENCE~~ SUMMARY
(Erase heading not required.)

Army Form C. 2118.

2nd Signal Squadron R.E.

Place	Date	Hour	Summary of Events and Information	Remarks and references to Appendices
LISESCOURT	9/1/17		3rd Machine Gun Sqdn line completed and working O.K. 9.30 Am	FW
			Supply Column line completed and working O.K. 1.15 Pm.	
			DOMPIERRE Trunk completed and working O.K. 4.45 Pm.	FW
	10TH		Usual Routine.	FW
	11TH		Lieut Smart of cavalry Corps signals started a course of Lectures to the Signal course.	FW
	12TH		A Sounder set was established and the squadron started to learn also course.	FW
	13TH		Usual Routine.	FW
	14TH		Usual Routine.	FW
	15TH		Usual Routine.	FW
	16th "		usual routine	
	17th "		Old cable line to O.C. A.S.C. at Dompierre picked up by course under instruction	FW
	18th "		Usual Routine	FW

2449 Wt. W14957/M90 750,000 1/16 J.B.C. & A. Forms/C.2118/12.

Instructions regarding War Diaries and Intelligence Summaries are contained in F. S. Regs., Part II. and the Staff Manual respectively. Title Pages will be prepared in manuscript.

WAR DIARY
or
~~INTELLIGENCE~~ SUMMARY
(Erase heading not required.)

Army Form C. 2118.

2nd Signal Squadron CC

Place	Date	Hour	Summary of Events and Information	Remarks and references to Appendices
	19/1/17		Usual routine — — —	FW
	20/1/17		— do — Buzzer and sounder test for Signal course	
	21/1/17		— do — — — — — — —	
	22nd		nothing to report. — — — — — — —	FW
	23rd		Class employed building a line from DOURIEZ to DOMINOIS —	FW
	24th		usual routine	FW
	25th		Signal class written exam in the morning	
	26th		usual routine. 2/Lt. Tuczek Essex Yeomanry attached temporary from Cavalry Corps Signals	FW
	27th		usual routine	FW
	28th		nothing to report	FW
	29th		Class, signalling to kite balloons	FW
	30th		Usual routine	FW
	31st		nothing to report	

F W Drake

Captain
XI Hussars

2449 Wt. W14957/M90 750,000 1/16 J.B.C. & A. Forms/C.2118/12.

CONFIDENTIAL.

Vol 19

WAR DIARY

OF

2nd SIGNAL SQUADRON, R.E.

FEBRUARY, 1917.
VOL. XXX.

============

Instructions regarding War Diaries and Intelligence Summaries are contained in F. S. Regs., Part II. and the Staff Manual respectively. Title Pages will be prepared in manuscript.

WAR DIARY
or
~~INTELLIGENCE SUMMARY~~
(Erase heading not required.)

Army Form C. 2118.

2nd Signal Squadron

Place	Date	Hour	Summary of Events and Information	Remarks and references to Appendices
LIGESCOURT	1/2/17		O.C. commenced course of wireless at Cavalry Corps signals, class under instruction carried out duties of Office staff, linemen etc.	FW
	2nd		as for 1st	FW
	3d		usual routine	FW
	4th "		nothing to report	FW
	5th & 6th		usual routine	
	7th "		Inspection of Squadron by A.D. Signals Cavalry Corps and French Officers of the French Cavalry Corps Signal service	FW
			Lecture by A.D.S. Cavalry Corps on the Signal Service	
	8th "		Usual routine	FW
	9th "		nothing to report	
	10th "		usual routine	FW
	11th "		—do—	
	12th "		—do—	
	13th "		Class examined in visual during morning, to Cavalry Corps Signals in the afternoon visiting Signal Office etc	FW
	14th "		Class, paper examination Course finished to-day	FW
	15th "		Officers & N.C.O's on the class returned to their regiments	

2449 Wt. W14957/M90 750,000 1/16 J.B.C. & A. Forms/C.2118/12.

Instructions regarding War Diaries and Intelligence Summaries are contained in F. S. Regs., Part II. and the Staff Manual respectively. Title Pages will be prepared in manuscript.

WAR DIARY
or
INTELLIGENCE SUMMARY

(Erase heading not required.)

Army Form C. 2118.

2nd Signal Squadron

Place	Date	Hour	Summary of Events and Information	Remarks and references to Appendices
LIGESCOURT	16/2/17		"A" Wireless detachment joined from Cavalry Corps Wireless Squadron. Mounted signallers and cyclists of the Squadron exercised on a visual scheme	FW
	17th		Routine as usual	FW
	18th		Usual routine	FW
	19th		All signallers exercised on visual scheme, Wireless detachment erecting station	FW
	20th		Usual routine. Despatch riders (3 from each Cavalry Brigade and 2 from the RHA) joined to-day	FW
	21st		Usual routine for Squadron. Despatch rider course commenced training	FW
	22nd		Usual routine	
	23rd		Squadron parade in marching order, Capt Nicholas RFC joined	FW
	24th		Usual routine, 3 men of R.F.C. joined	
	25th		Usual routine	[illegible]
	26th		Work on new line in new 4th Cav. Bde. area	[illegible]
	27th		same as 26th	
	28th		— " — D.R. course finished and men returned to their Regiments	[illegible]

[signature] Lieut 12th R Lancers
for O.C. 2nd Signal Squadron

2449 Wt. W14957/M90 750,000 1/16 J.B.C. & A. Forms/C.2118/12.

CONFIDENTIAL.

Vol 20

WAR DIARY

OF

2nd SIGNAL SQUADRON, R.E.

MARCH, 1917.

VOL. XXXI.

Army Form C. 2118.

Instructions regarding War Diaries and Intelligence Summaries are contained in F. S. Regs., Part II. and the Staff Manual respectively. Title Pages will be prepared in manuscript.

WAR DIARY
or
~~INTELLIGENCE SUMMARY~~
(Erase heading not required.)

2d Signal Squadron R.E.

Place	Date	Hour	Summary of Events and Information	Remarks and references to Appendices
LIGESCOURT	1/3/17		R.H.A. course of signalling commenced	H.D.
	2nd.		Picking up old ~~4 Cav Bde~~ Supply Column line, usual routine	H.D.
	3d		Usual routine, work on lines in new 4th Cav Bde. area	H.D.
	4th "		nothing to report. — do —	H.D.
	5th "		usual routine	F.W.
	6th "		— do —	F.W.
	7th "		— do —	F.W.
	8th "		nothing to report.	F.W.
	9th "		Scheme aeroplane communication from ground	F.W.
	10th "		usual routine	F.W.
	11th "		usual routine	F.W.
	12th "		2d D.R. course commenced attended by 1 man per regiment of the Division and 3 from the R.H.A.	F.W.
	13th "		usual routine	F.W.
	14th "		Usual routine	F.W.
	15th "		Signalling scheme	F.W.
	16th "		Nothing to report	F.W.

2449 Wt. W14957/M90 750,000 1/16 J.B.C. & A. Forms/C.2118/12.

Instructions regarding War Diaries and Intelligence Summaries are contained in F. S. Regs., Part II. and the Staff Manual respectively. Title Pages will be prepared in manuscript.

WAR DIARY
or
INTELLIGENCE SUMMARY
(Erase heading not required.)

Army Form C. 2118.

2nd Signal Squadron
2nd Cavalry Division

Place	Date	Hour	Summary of Events and Information	Remarks and references to Appendices
LIGESCOURT	17th		Aeroplane scheme in morning	
	18th		Nothing to report	
	19th		— do —	
	20th		Captain Nicholas left, Capt Mosley-Leigh joined. Wireless detachment exercised in erecting pack & trench sets working to 2 C.O. and P.C. D.R. Course completed and men returned to regiments	
	21st		Nothing to report 2/Lt Turczek returned to Cavalry Corps	
	22d		Nothing to report	
	23rd		Divisional scheme, following methods of communication employed, visual, wireless, aeroplanes	
	24th		Usual routine	
	25th		— do —	
	26th		— do —	
	27th		nothing to report	
	28th		usual routine	
	29th		— do —	

Army Form C. 2118.

Instructions regarding War Diaries and Intelligence Summaries are contained in F. S. Regs., Part II. and the Staff Manual respectively. Title Pages will be prepared in manuscript.

WAR DIARY
or
~~INTELLIGENCE SUMMARY~~

(Erase heading not required.)

2d Signal Squadron

Place	Date	Hour	Summary of Events and Information	Remarks and references to Appendices
LIGESCOURT	30/3/17		Marching order parade for inspection by the Divisional Commander	[initials]
	31st.		Nothing to report	

[signature]
Captain
XI Hussars
Cmdg 2d Signal Sqdn

2449 Wt. W14957/M90 750,000 1/16 J.B.C. & A. Forms/C.2118/12.

Vol 21

CONFIDENTIAL.

WAR DIARY

of

2nd SIGNAL SQUADRON, R.E.

APRIL, 1917.

VOL. XXXII.

Instructions regarding War Diaries and Intelligence Summaries are contained in F. S. Regs., Part II. and the Staff Manual respectively. Title pages will be prepared in manuscript.

WAR DIARY
or
~~INTELLIGENCE SUMMARY.~~
(Erase heading not required.)

2nd Signal Squadron RE

Army Form C. 2118.

Place	Date	Hour	Summary of Events and Information	Remarks and references to Appendices
	APRIL			
LIGESCOURT	1		Usual routine	HW
	2		-do-	HW
	3		-do-	HW
	4		-do-	HW
	5		3rd Cav. Bde. moved from TORTEFONTAINE to OCCOCHES communication only by D.R.	HW
			4th -"- -"- moved from QUEND LE JEUNE to DOMONOIS communication by telegraph and telephone on old Divisional school line	
			5th -"- -"- moved from GROFFLIERS to TORTEFONTAINE took over old PC office	
			One Officer and 50 other ranks (dismounted party) joined to recover wire etc. on Division leaving area	
	6		All moves postponed for 24 hours	HW
CHATEAU DE BEAUVOIR	7		Squadron moved from LIGESCOURT 8AM. Signal office closed at 11AM and reopened at CHATEAU DE BEAUVOIR same hour, morse direct to C.A.R. and by telephone via DOULLENS exchange. Communication to 3rd Cav Bde at MONPLAISIER, 4TH Cav. Bde at FROHEM-LE-GRANDE, 5TH Cav. Bde. at OUTREBOIS by M/C. D.R. only. Local subscribers GS. + Q.	HW

T2134. Wt. W708-776. 500000. 4/15. Sir J. C. & S.

Instructions regarding War Diaries and Intelligence Summaries are contained in F. S. Regs., Part II. and the Staff Manual respectively. Title pages will be prepared in manuscript.

WAR DIARY
or
~~INTELLIGENCE SUMMARY.~~
(Erase heading not required.)

Army Form C. 2118.

2d Signal Squadron RE

Place	Date	Hour	Summary of Events and Information	Remarks and references to Appendices
	APRIL			
HENU	8	10AM	Squadron moved	FW
		12 MD	Forward office opened, back office at CHATEAU DE BEAUVOIR closed same hour	
			Communication to Z.C.O. at DUISANS direct by telegraph and telephone	
		2PM	" to P.C. at GAUDIEMPRE " " "	
			" to PD at PAS " telephone only	
			" to PE at WANINCOURT " telegraph and telephone	
			" to E.C.O. sub exchange at ACHEUX	
			Local subscribers GS + Q.	
	9	9.30AM	Division moved, rendezvous at POMMIER. all communication by D.R.	FW
			Office at HENU closed at 9.30am opened at RONVILLE same hour.	
		2PM	Advanced Divisional report centre opened at G 34 b (cross roads) through to ZERO by phone	
		8PM	this office closed	
		2.30PM	Dwl report centre moved to M 6 c central, cme to Z.C.P. by phone about 4.30pm to PC, PD, PE by visual and mounted D.R.	
		8.30PM	Dwl. report centre closed and reopened at AGNY about 12 midnight	

T2134. Wt. W708–776. 500000. 4/15. Sir J. C. & S.

Instructions regarding War Diaries and Intelligence Summaries are contained in F. S. Regs., Part II. and the Staff Manual respectively. Title pages will be prepared in manuscript.

WAR DIARY
or
~~INTELLIGENCE SUMMARY.~~
(*Erase heading not required.*)

Army Form C. 2118.

2d Signal Squadron RE

Place	Date	Hour	Summary of Events and Information	Remarks and references to Appendices
	APRIL			
AGNY	9		Communication only by M/C D.R. Wireless wagon broke down in WAILLY during the afternoon, whole wireless detachment left there in village	
	10	6 AM	Cmn. established with Z.C.O. via Kite balloon circuit.	
		10.30 AM	Report centre moved to cross roads G.34.b. D.R. cmn, only remained there about ¼ an hour then moved to M.6.c. central.	
		2.30 pm	Cmn. with Z.C.P. by phone and with Brigades by visual and mounted D.R.	
		5 pm	3rd Cav Bde moved to N.14.a 5th Cav. Bde. to two visual transmitting stations placed on TELEGRAPH HILL who maintained cmn. between Divl. report centre and forward Brigades, mounted D.R.s employed as snow-storms often prevented visual work. Two Brigades remained in these positions all night	
		7.30 pm	Cmn. opened from G.34.b to ZERO by telephone	
		8 PM	Divl. report centre returned to G.34.b.	
	11th.	4.30 AM	Cmn. opened by phone with Z.C.P. from M.6.c, office at G.34.b remained open	
		1 PM	Morse est. at G.34.b through to ZERO closed at 4 PM and moved back to AGNY Visual worked from M.6.c. central to PC + PE. 2 transmitters employed to PC, one to PE. The Aldis lamp was used to attract the attention of both	

Instructions regarding War Diaries and Intelligence Summaries are contained in F. S. Regs., Part II. and the Staff Manual respectively. Title pages will be prepared in manuscript.

WAR DIARY
or
~~INTELLIGENCE SUMMARY.~~
(Erase heading not required.)

Army Form C. 2118.

2d Signal Squadron R.E.

Place	Date	Hour	Summary of Events and Information	Remarks and references to Appendices
	APRIL			
	11		Brigades, flags at first could not be discerned, with lamp in each case cmc was opened at once	
		6 PM.	Report centre moved, returning to AGNY	
			Wireless wagon and detachment rejoined to-day new rear portion being sent from Wireless Z.C.O.	FW
		7 PM	Cmc opened with Z.C.O at DUISANS, 3d Cav. Bde at AGNY 4th + 5th at WAILLY by DR.	
AGNY	12	1 PM	Office closed, reopened at HENU chateau at 3.30 pm to Z.C.O. by telegraph and telephone, M/C. DR.s to all Brigades	FW
		2 PM	Squadron moved from AGNY to HENU	
HENU	13th		Cmc. to PC + PE by telegraph and telephone at GUADIEMPRE and WANINCOURT respectively and by telephone only to P.D. at PAS, cmc. also est to V.D. at MARIEUX direct by telephone, ZCO - VB - VD. morse circuit.	FW
	14th		cmc. established to V.D. by telegraph	FW
	15th		Usual routine	FW
	16th		20th Hussars bridged across P.E. pair	FW
	17th		Usual routine	

T2134. Wt. W708—776. 500000. 4/15. Sir J. C. & S.

Instructions regarding War Diaries and Intelligence Summaries are contained in F. S. Regs., Part II. and the Staff Manual respectively. Title pages will be prepared in manuscript.

WAR DIARY
or
~~INTELLIGENCE SUMMARY.~~

(*Erase heading not required.*)

2nd Signal Squadron RE

Army Form C. 2118.

Place	Date	Hour	Summary of Events and Information	Remarks and references to Appendices
	APRIL			
HENU	18	11.40 AM	Field Squadron put on to exchange	
	19		2d Cav. Bde moved, billet at FROHEM-LE-GRANDE cmc through P.D. at PAS. by telephone	
	20		P.C. move to VAULX cmc. only by D.R. PE moved to FROHEM LE GRANDE cmc by morse and telephone. 2nd Dragoons remain at LUCHEUX cmc by telegraph & telephone.	
	21st.		Through to PAS exchange on phone as additional outlet	
	22.		Nothing to report	
	23		-do-	
	24		~~Throughto~~ P.C. transmitted via PE.	
	25		Usual routine	
	26		Usual routine A.S.C. put on exchange	
	27		Nothing to report	
	28	9AM	Squadron parade and move to FROHEM LE GRANDE. cmc with C.A.R. & P.D. by 12 30 to PC & PE all on morse and phone by 3pm. Local circuits G.S. & Q	
	29		A.S.C. RHA 7 Field Squadron cmc ~~by~~ via P.D. exchange	
	30		Nothing to report.	

[signature] Captain
XI Hussars
Cmdg 2d Signal Squadron

T2134. Wt. W708–776. 500000. 4/15. Sir J. C. & S.

Vol 22

CONFIDENTIAL.

WAR DIARY

of

2nd SIGNAL SQUADRON, R.E.

VOL. XXXIII.

MAY, 1917.

Instructions regarding War Diaries and Intelligence Summaries are contained in F. S. Regs., Part II. and the Staff Manual respectively. Title pages will be prepared in manuscript.

WAR DIARY
or
~~INTELLIGENCE SUMMARY.~~
(Erase heading not required.)

2nd Signal Squadron

Army Form C. 2118.

Place	Date	Hour	Summary of Events and Information	Remarks and references to Appendices
	MAY			
FROHEM LE GRANDE	1		Usual routine	FW
	2		-do- A.S.C. put on exchange	FW
	3		-do- Signallers of Squadron + Bde Sig Trps. exercised in sending messages by Aldis lam to Kite balloon	FW
	4		-do- -do-	FW
	5-8		Usual routine	FW
	9		Divisional Commander inspected Signal office, billets, stables + horses.	FW
	10-11		Usual routine	
ST OUEN	12		Squadron march 8AM to ST OUEN office opened 11 AM there, back office closed same hour communication to L of C office DOMART by morse + phone, E.A.R. on morse with DOMART intermediate, to PC on phone at FROHEM LE GRANDE + PD at MOLLIENS-AU-BOIS, to PE by D.R. only. Local offices G.S, Q + ASC. 2/Lt JOHNSON IV HSRS. joined for duty.	FW
BUSSY LES DAOURS	13		Squadron march at 8AM to BUSSY LES DAOURS communication to DAOURS intermediate + D.A.R. sub office at QUERRIEU by morse + phone, PE at QUERRIEU operators supplied by them for working office, on phone to PD at FOUILLOY via CORBIE exchange, to PC by DR, only, on phone to C.R.H.A. at AUBIGNY, locals G.S + Q	FW

T2134. Wt. W708–776. 500000. 4/15. Sir J. C. & S.

Instructions regarding War Diaries and Intelligence Summaries are contained in F. S. Regs., Part II. and the Staff Manual respectively. Title pages will be prepared in manuscript.

WAR DIARY
or
~~INTELLIGENCE SUMMARY.~~
(Erase heading not required.)

Army Form C. 2118.

2nd Signal Squadron

Place	Date	Hour	Summary of Events and Information	Remarks and references to Appendices
	MAY			
LAMOTTE EN SANTERRE	14		Squadron march to LAMOTTE EN SANTERRE, on morse and phone to DAR sub office at VILLERS LE BRITONNEUX, to PD at BAYONVILLERS to PC at QUERRIEU, to PE by DR. only	[illegible initials]
K.10.C.0.8.	15		Squadron march 7 AM to K.10.C.0.8. communication to 42ND Division at K11.a.7.9 reference sheet 62c cme to Bdes by D.R only	APB
	16		Usual routine Lieut Brand 12th Lancers posted to 4th Sig Trp. 26 men from VC. 1 officer 8 men PF. 9 men PG, 1 officer 8 men PH attached	APB
	17		-do-	APB
	18		-do- 2/Lt Macintyre, Cav Corps. Signals attached	APB
K.11.A.7.9.	19		Office ~~opened~~ in Quarry at K11.A.7.9. taken over from 42ND Division at 9AM. cme by phone only to 9S. Q. CRA, CRE, ADMS, RE dump, (OC ASC + DADOS at K.10.C.0.4.) I.H. Right group Artillery at ST EMILIE, V.F 5th Cav Bde at K.32.b.10.7. morse + phone to Res Bde 42nd Div 125th Bde. at VILLERS FAUCON, 3rd Cav Bde. at EPEHY F.1.D.7.8, 4th Cav Bde at ST EMILIE at E24.b.9.9. 5th Cav Bde. TINCOURT J.23.b.6.6, Cav Corps at CATELET	APB
	20		Following additions to yesterday, on morse + phone to 2/6 Sherwood Foresters at VILLERS-FAUCON who accept for M.G.E. in same village phone only	APB

T2134. Wt. W708–776. 500000. 4/15. Sir J. C. & S.

Instructions regarding War Diaries and Intelligence Summaries are contained in F. S. Regs., Part II. and the Staff Manual respectively. Title pages will be prepared in manuscript.

WAR DIARY
or
~~INTELLIGENCE SUMMARY.~~
(Erase heading not required.)

Army Form C. 2118.

2d Signal Squadron

Place	Date	Hour	Summary of Events and Information	Remarks and references to Appendices
	MAY			
	21st		MGE. 5th Machine Gun Sqdn took over office at VILLERS-FAUCON from 2/8 SHERWOODS who moved to SAULCOURT cme to MGE morse and telephone, cme to 2/8 SHERWOODS through MGE.	APB
	22		All subscribers put on 24 line board and separate Artillery exchange done away with	APB
	23rd to 25th		Usual routine, improving existing lines and clearing up area, personnel attached from 3d Cavalry Division left and returned to their units	APB APB
	26		3d Cav. Bde. relieved by 6th Cav. Bde. and go into Billets at TINCOURT communication by morse with P.E. intermediate, telephone via PE exchange on morse & telephone to V.C.R. (3d Cav. Divn. advanced) at VILLERS-FAUCON	APB APB.
	27th to 31st.		Improving existing lines replacing where necessary and clearing up locally	APB.

A. P. Bodnett (?) Captain
XI Hussars
Cmdg 2d Signal Squadron

T2134. Wt. W708—776. 500000. 4/15. Sir J. C. & S.

W.O. 95 / 1123

CONFIDENTIAL

War Diary
of
2nd Signal Squadron R.E.
From 1/6/17 To 30/6/17

Volume XXXIV

Instructions regarding War Diaries and Intelligence Summaries are contained in F. S. Regs., Part II. and the Staff Manual respectively. Title pages will be prepared in manuscript.

WAR DIARY
or
~~INTELLIGENCE SUMMARY.~~
(Erase heading not required.)

Army Form C. 2118.

2nd Signal Squadron R.E.

Place	Date	Hour	Summary of Events and Information	Remarks and references to Appendices
	JUNE			
K.11.a.7.9.	1		5th Cavalry Brigade took over portion of the line held by the 4th Cavalry Bde on night of 31st/1st. 4th C B go into billets at BRUSLE, communication by morse and phone via Z.C.O. and P.G. Town major VILLERS FAUCON put on phone	FW
	2.		Nothing to report	FW
	3		-do- usual line maintenance and recovering derelict cable etc	FW
	4.		Z.C.O. (Cavalry Corps) working party ran a pair from ROMA exchange to V.B. office ROMA now put through to 14 R.F.S. and led into this office for testing purposes	FW
	5		Through to QUARRIES on direct pair at 11.30 pm LIEUT. WARNEFORD 7th D.G.s joined for duty	FW
	6		Nothing to report	FW
	7		LIEUT. A.P BODEN (M.C) 12TH. R. LANCERS left on being posted to 7th Signal Troop RE	FW
	8		Main trunk to ST EMILIE smashed by shell fire near VILLERS FAUCON about 4 45 pm working O.K. at 6pm	FW
	9		Nothing to report	FW
	10		Through to (V.D.R.) 4th Cavalry Division on phone at K.24.a.1.0. direct pair	FW
	11		~~Recovering~~ usual line maintenance and recovering cable	FW

T2134. Wt. W708-776. 500000. 4/15. Sir J. C. & S.

Army Form C. 2118.

Instructions regarding War Diaries and Intelligence Summaries are contained in F. S. Regs., Part II. and the Staff Manual respectively. Title pages will be prepared in manuscript.

WAR DIARY
or
~~INTELLIGENCE SUMMARY.~~
(Erase heading not required.)

2d Signal Squadron RE

Place	Date	Hour	Summary of Events and Information	Remarks and references to Appendices
	JUNE			
K.11.a.7.9.	12		All telephone communication in front of fighting Brigades Head Qrs stopped by Divisional Commanders orders for 12 hours, only visual stations and runners employed. This worked without a hitch.	FW
	13		Line run from forward Brigade to M.G.S. at ST EMILIE	FW
	14		Nothing to report	FW
	15		3d C Brigade "BELLS" Bde relieved 5th Cav Brigade "CHAS" Bde in the line at change carried out satisfactorily	FW
	16		DI twin lateral between QUARRIES and Right regiment replaced by D5 twin. Pigeon messages now coming in satisffactorily, average time 14 minutes from advanced posts	FW
	17		Second power buzzer put into "B" post during night working back to amplifyer in sunken road.	FW
	18		All DI cable picked up in right sub sector and replaced by DV. All telephones disconnected and lines put to earth from 3.15 PM to 3.45pm on account of thunder storm, morse working as usual	FW
	19		All telephone communication cut of between hours of 7.12AM to 7.25AM and 12.12pm to 12.50pm	FW

T2134. Wt. W708–776. 500000. 4/15. Sir J. C. & S.

Instructions regarding War Diaries and Intelligence Summaries are contained in F. S. Regs., Part II. and the Staff Manual respectively. Title pages will be prepared in manuscript.

WAR DIARY
or
~~INTELLIGENCE SUMMARY.~~
(*Erase heading not required.*)

Army Form C. 2118.

2nd Signal Squadron R.E.

Place	Date	Hour	Summary of Events and Information	Remarks and references to Appendices
	JUNE			
K11.a.7.9.	19		on account of thunder storms	[illegible]
	20		Nothing to report	[illegible]
	21.		Usual routine. After heavy shelling by Germans GILLEMONT FARM attacked	[illegible]
	~~22~~		all lines were cut, base line of Power buzzer was cut with the result that very weak signals were obtained at amplifyer.	
	22.		Nothing to report.	[illegible]
	23		Recovering cable, and work on local lines	
	24		Nothing to report.	
	25		Usual routine	
	26		— do —	
	27		— do —	
	28		4th Cavalry Brigade took over from 3d Cavalry Brigade	
	29		3d Cavalry Brigade took over from 6th Cavalry Brigade therefore making communications of two Cavalry Divisions into one. this office remains same place.	
	30.		Nothing to report. Sapper Bell attached from Signals Car Corps.	

T2134. Wt. W708—776. 500000. 4/15. Sir J. C. & S.

Vol 24

CONFIDENTIAL

War Diary
of

2d Signal Squadron RE

From 1st July to 31st July 1917

Volume XXXV

Instructions regarding War Diaries and Intelligence Summaries are contained in F. S. Regs., Part II. and the Staff Manual respectively. Title pages will be prepared in manuscript.

WAR DIARY
or
~~INTELLIGENCE SUMMARY.~~
(Erase heading not required.)

Army Form C. 2118.

2nd Signal Squadron R.E.

Place	Date JULY	Hour	Summary of Events and Information	Remarks and references to Appendices
K11a.7.9	1		Nothing to report	FW
	2		Line patrols and usual maintanance	FW
	3		-do- -do-	FW
	4	AM 12.30	Attack on GILLEMONT FARM by Oxford Hussars all lines held throughout	FW
	5		Germans heavily shelled GILLEMONT FARM all lines cut, power buzzer kept going and sent through two code messages, as soon as shelling ceased line again restored	FW
	6		Lines were constructed at COURCELLES for use of Division when moving to next area	FW
	7		4th Cavalry Bde relieved by 106th Infantry Bde, all communications same as before. All wireless instruments left in line and taken over by 106th Bde. 2d Cav Div Pack set remains in position	FW
	8		Nothing to report	FW
	9		Squadron moved to COURCELLES Office closed at K11a.7.9. 11AM and reopened COURCELLES same hour. communication to Cavalry Corps by	FW

Instructions regarding War Diaries and Intelligence Summaries are contained in F. S. Regs., Part II. and the Staff Manual respectively. Title pages will be prepared in manuscript.

WAR DIARY
or
~~INTELLIGENCE SUMMARY.~~
(Erase heading not required.)

2d Signal Squadron RE.

Army Form C. 2118.

Place	Date	Hour	Summary of Events and Information	Remarks and references to Appendices
	JULY			
COURCELLES	9		telegraph & telephone to 3rd Cav. Bde & 5th Cav Bde at TINCOURT both direct with PC intermediate. Cavalry Corps transmitted work to 4th Cav Bde at BRUSLE. Local offices G S & Q	WfW
	10		Cavalry Corps came in intermediate to 4th Cavalry Bde.	WfW
	11		Nothing to report.	WfW
	12		4th. Cavalry Bde move to Chateau on main road N of A in CAPPY communication by DR only 5th Cavalry Bde move to SUZANNE, cavalry corps intermediate. 3d Cav. Bde. unchanged.	WfW
	13		Squadron move to SUZANNE communication to 3d & 5th Cavalry Bdes at CAPPY and TREUX respectively morse & phone, To 4th Cavalry Bde by DR only at HEILLY, to Cavalry Corps at LE CATLET direct by morse & phone. Office opened at 11 AM	WfW
	14		Squadron moved to TREUX office closed at SUZANNE at 11 AM reopened at TREUX same hour, communication to Cavalry Corps at LE CATLET by morse, by morse & phone to 3d Cav. Bde at HEILLY, by DR to 4th Cav Bde at AMPLIER, circulation through them to 5th Cavalry Bde	WfW

Instructions regarding War Diaries and Intelligence Summaries are contained in F. S. Regs., Part II. and the Staff Manual respectively. Title pages will be prepared in manuscript.

WAR DIARY
or
~~INTELLIGENCE~~ SUMMARY.
(Erase heading not required.)

2d Signal Squadron RE

Army Form C. 2118.

Place	Date	Hour	Summary of Events and Information	Remarks and references to Appendices
	JULY			
	15		Office closed at TREUX at 11AM reopened at MARIEUX same hour communication to Cavalry Corps via 3d Army. all communication to Brigades by D.R. 3d Cav Bde at ORVILLE. 4th 5th Cavalry Bdes in ETREE WAMIN area	[initials]
	16		Office closed at 11AM reopened at HOUVIN-HOUVIGNEUL same hour communication to 5th Cavalry Bde at WAMIN by morse & telephone, telegraph & telephone to FREVENT & telegraph to AVESNES.	[initials]
HOUVIN	17th		Through to 3rd Cav. Bde at REBREUVIETTE by morse & phone to 4th Cavalry Bde by telephone only at VACQUERIE-LE-BOUCQ	[initials]
	18th		Through to Cavalry Corps at AIRE direct by morse & phone	[initials]
	19th to 22nd		Nothing to report. usual routine	[initials]
	23rd		3d Cavalry Brigade moved to REBREUVE chateau, work transmitted through 5th Cav Bde office	[initials]
	24th		Usual routine	[initials]
	25-29		Nothing to report. R.F.C. personnel joined on 28th.	[initials]
	30		5th Cav Bde move to FROHEM-LE-GRAND telegraphic communication via 3d Cav Bde office. Telephone 3d Cav Bde, FREVENT and DOULLENS Supply Column brought on to FREVENT exchange	[initials]

T2134. Wt. W708—776. 500000. 4/15. Sir J. C. & S.

Army Form C. 2118.

Instructions regarding War Diaries and Intelligence Summaries are contained in F. S. Regs., Part II. and the Staff Manual respectively. Title pages will be prepared in manuscript.

WAR DIARY
or
~~INTELLIGENCE SUMMARY.~~
(Erase heading not required.)

2d Signal Squadron RE

Place	Date	Hour	Summary of Events and Information	Remarks and references to Appendices
	JULY			
HOUVIN	31		Usual routine	

[illegible] Captain
XI Hussars
Cmdg 2d Signal Squadron
RE

T2134. Wt. W708–776. 500000. 4/15. Sir J. C. & S.

Vol 25

Confidential

War Diary

of

2nd Signal Squadron RE

From 1/8/17 to 31/8/17

Volume. XXXVI

Army Form C. 2118.

WAR DIARY
~~or~~
~~INTELLIGENCE SUMMARY~~.
(*Erase heading not required.*)

2nd Signal Squadron RE

Instructions regarding War Diaries and Intelligence Summaries are contained in F. S. Regs., Part II. and the Staff Manual respectively. Title pages will be prepared in manuscript.

Place	Date	Hour	Summary of Events and Information	Remarks and references to Appendices
	AUGUST			
HOUVIN -	1		Through to 5th Cavalry Brigade on morse direct on phone via FREVENT	FW
HOUVIGNEUL			and DOULLENS exchanges.	FW
	2		usual routine	
	3 & 4		Local circuits replaced by airline, cable collected in	FW
	5		usual routine	FW
	6		Cable from main route to 5th Cavalry Brigade replaced by airline	
	7 & 8		Line maintanance etc	FW
	9		Usual routine	
	10		Line maintanance etc	FW
	11		O.C. A.C. at HOUVIGNEUL put on phone	
	12 & 13		Usual routine	FW
	14		Usual routine all dismounted men instructed in line work, jointing etc	
	15 & 16		Same as 14th ~~mounted party~~ all Signallers Flag drill & station	FW.
			work during afternoon	
	17-19		Usual routine	FW
	20		— " — Signalling and line instruction to operators	FW

T2134. Wt. W708-776. 500000. 4/15. Sir J. C. & S.

Instructions regarding War Diaries and Intelligence Summaries are contained in F. S. Regs., Part II. and the Staff Manual respectively. Title pages will be prepared in manuscript.

WAR DIARY
or
~~INTELLIGENCE~~ SUMMARY.
(Erase heading not required.)

Army Form C. 2118.

2d Signal Squadron RE

Place	Date	Hour	Summary of Events and Information	Remarks and references to Appendices
HOUVIN– HOUVIGNEUL	August 21st		Captain F. V. Drake XI Hrs departed to U.K. on Leave	ACM
	22nd		Usual Routine.	[illegible]
	23rd		Training of Visual Signallers in the afternoon.	ACM
	24th		Usual Routine.	ACM
	25th		Usual Routine	ACM
	26th		Sunday no training	ACM
	27th		Held class of instruction in line building. Weather very stormy.	ACM
	28th		From 8 Am until 4 Pm strong gale blowing, all lines to Cavalry Corps 3rd 4th and 5th Brigades were either down or faulty chiefly caused by falling trees the last fault on Cavalry Corps line which ~~[illegible]~~ is thirty miles long was cleared at 5.30 Pm. Line built to 3rd Brigade R.H.A.	ACM
	29th		Severe weather much rain and wind during day but not so much trouble on lines as yesterday	ACM

T2134. Wt. W708–776. 500000. 4/15. Sir J. C. & S.

Instructions regarding War Diaries and Intelligence Summaries are contained in F. S. Regs., Part II. and the Staff Manual respectively. Title pages will be prepared in manuscript.

WAR DIARY
or
~~INTELLIGENCE SUMMARY.~~
(Erase heading not required.)

Army Form C. 2118.

2nd Signal Squadron R.E.

Place	Date	Hour	Summary of Events and Information	Remarks and references to Appendices
HOUVIN-HOUVIGNEUL	Aug 30th		Hut for Canteen was built.	[illegible]
	31st		Canteen opened.	[illegible]

[illegible signature] 2nd Lieut
for Captain
Cmdg 2nd Signal Squadron R.E.

31/8/17

Vol 26

Confidential
War Diary
of
2d Signal Squadron R.E.
From September 1st 1917
To September 30th 1917

Volume XXXVII

Instructions regarding War Diaries and Intelligence Summaries are contained in F. S. Regs., Part II. and the Staff Manual respectively. Title pages will be prepared in manuscript.

WAR DIARY
or
~~INTELLIGENCE SUMMARY.~~
(Erase heading not required.)

Army Form C. 2118.

2nd Signal Squadron RE

Place	Date	Hour	Summary of Events and Information	Remarks and references to Appendices
HOUVIN-HOUVIGNEUL	Sept			
	1st		Usual Routine	ACWL
	2		Line instruction to operators and Pioneers, visual Signalling	FW
	3		-do- -do-	
	4		Signalling scheme (visual)	FW
	5		Line instruction etc.	FW
	6		Class commenced for men of Signal Troops line construction, instruments etc.	FW
	7		Scheme visual signallers and mounted D.R's employed, night scheme with lamps (visual) and DR's. Lt Johnson IV Hrs went to RHA in the line	FW
	8		Signal + DR scheme	FW
	9		Nothing to report	
	10		Line + instrument instruction to men from Sig Tps.	FW
	11		-do- -do-	
	12		As for the 11th Signallers employed on visual Scheme	FW
	13		Class under instruction finished and men returned to Signal Troops	FW
	14		Visual Signal scheme in afternoon	
	15		Usual routine O.C. attended conference of A.D Signals + Squadron leaders at ST POL	FW

Instructions regarding War Diaries and Intelligence Summaries are contained in F. S. Regs., Part II. and the Staff Manual respectively. Title pages will be prepared in manuscript.

WAR DIARY
or
~~INTELLIGENCE SUMMARY.~~
(Erase heading not required.)

Army Form C. 2118.

2d Signal Squadron R.E.

Place	Date	Hour	Summary of Events and Information	Remarks and references to Appendices
	September			
HOUVIN - HOUVIGNEUL	16.		Usual routine LIEUT WARNEFORD ordered to HAVRE to superintend making of proposed blanket hold	[illegible]
	17		Usual routine	[illegible]
	18		Squadron exercise mounted	[illegible]
	19		Usual routine	[illegible]
	20		Usual routine. O.C visited 3rd Bde RHA in the line	[illegible]
	21		Usual routine, Line maintenance	[illegible]
	22		Nothing to report	[illegible]
	23		Usual routine	[illegible]
	24		-do-	[illegible]
	25		Squadron exercise, mounted, individual riding	[illegible]
	26		Usual routine. O.C visited 3rd Cav. Bde. classification of Signallers	[illegible]
	27th		Nothing to report	
	28		Aeroplane scheme at 3d Cav Bde resulted in failure as machine crashed in landing	
	29 & 30		Usual routine	[illegible]

[illegible signature] for Captain, Comdg. Signals, 2nd Cavalry Division.

Vol 27

Confidential

War Diary

of

2nd Signal Squadron RE

From 1/10/17 to 31/10/17

Vol No XXXVIII

Instructions regarding War Diaries and Intelligence Summaries are contained in F. S. Regs., Part II. and the Staff Manual respectively. Title pages will be prepared in manuscript.

WAR DIARY
or
~~INTELLIGENCE SUMMARY.~~
(Erase heading not required.)

Army Form C. 2118.

2nd Signal Squadron RE

Place	Date	Hour	Summary of Events and Information	Remarks and references to Appendices
	OCTOBER			
HOUVIN	1		Nothing to report	FW
HOUVIGNEUL	2-7		Usual routine, line maintenance	FW
HEUCHIN	8	8AM	Squadron march from HOUVIN · HOUVIGNEUL to HEUCHIN back office closed 12 noon new office opened same hour, through by phone to (ZCO) Cavalry Corps at AIRE, PD 4th Cavalry Bde at MONCHY-CAYEUX, PE 5th Cavalry Bde at SAUTRECOURT all at 11.30 AM, locals GS & Q. ZCO on by morse at 12 noon; 12.25 pm morse to PE, 1.5 pm to PD, (PC) 3d Cavalry Bde on by phone at 12.55 pm via PE and 1.30 pm morse	FW
	9		2/Lieut JOHNSON IV Hrs & 3 linemen rejoined from 3d Bde RHA. O.C visited Brigades	FW
	10/11		Improving existing circuits and lines to Brigades	FW
	12		O.C visited AD Signals	
	13		Usual routine. improving Brigade lines	FW
	14		Nothing to report	
	15		Usual routine. O.C visited 4th & 5th Brigade Troops	FW
	16		Usual routine	
	17		Nothing to report	

Instructions regarding War Diaries and Intelligence Summaries are contained in F. S. Regs., Part II. and the Staff Manual respectively. Title pages will be prepared in manuscript.

WAR DIARY
or
~~INTELLIGENCE SUMMARY.~~
(Erase heading not required.)

2nd Signal Squadron RE

Army Form C. 2118.

Place	Date	Hour	Summary of Events and Information	Remarks and references to Appendices
	OCTOBER			
HEUCHIN	18		5th Cav. Bde moved to REBREUVE communication by DR. only	
	19		HQ Staff and Signal Office staff remain at HEUCHIN remainder of Squadron move to HOUVIN HOUVIGNEUL. 4th Cavalry Brigade move to REBREUVE. 5th Cavalry Brigade to DOMART-en Ponthieu all communication to 4th & 5th Bdes by DR. only.	
	20		5th Cav. Bde moved to LUXIERE. 4th Cav. Bde to DOMART. Signal Squadron at ST HILIARE. 3d Cav. Bde. move to REBREUVE. Divisional H.Q. and Signal Office staff move from HEUCHIN to ST-SAUFLIEU. cmc. to all Brigades by DR only, to Cavalry Corps at BEAUQUESNES by morse direct and by telephone via AMIENS	
			V.B. Office in French civil office, locals GS & Q	
	21		Squadron marched to ST-SAUFLIEU, 4th Cavalry Brigade moved to SAINS-EN-AMIENOIS communication by phone at 3.25pm. ~~4th~~ 3rd Cav. Bde. move to DOMART communication by DR. only	
	22		3d Cavalry Brigade move to CREUSE cmc. by DR. only. O.C. visited Brigades. Telegraph cmc to 4th Cavalry Bde. To 5th.	

T2134. Wt. W708—776. 500000. 4/15. Sir J. C. & S.

Instructions regarding War Diaries and Intelligence Summaries are contained in F. S. Regs., Part II. and the Staff Manual respectively. Title pages will be prepared in manuscript.

WAR DIARY

or

~~INTELLIGENCE SUMMARY.~~

(Erase heading not required.)

Army Form C. 2118.

2nd Signal Squadron RE

Place	Date	Hour	Summary of Events and Information	Remarks and references to Appendices
	OCTOBER			
ST-SAUFLIEU	22		5th Cavalry Bde by phone via AMIENS, CONTY + CONTRE all French civil ADMS and ASC put on phone	[initials]
	23		Supply Column put on SALEUX civil exchange. Signal office moved from civil office to room behind	[initials]
	24		Usual routine	[initials]
	25		Nothing to report	
	26		usual routine	[initials]
	27			
	28			
	29		Detachment No 5 Construction party arrived to build lines in this area commenced building line to NAMPTY in the afternoon	[initials]
	30		Work on line to NAMPTY continued	[initials]
	31		as for 30th	

[signature] Captain
XI Hussars
Comdg 2d Signal Squadron

T2134. Wt. W708–776. 500000. 4/15. Sir J. C. & S.

Vol 28

War Diary
of
2nd Signal Squadron R.E.

From 1/11/17 to 30/11/17

Vol. No XXXIX

Instructions regarding War Diaries and Intelligence Summaries are contained in F. S. Regs., Part II. and the Staff Manual respectively. Title pages will be prepared in manuscript.

WAR DIARY
~~or~~
~~INTELLIGENCE SUMMARY.~~
(Erase heading not required.)

Army Form C. 2118.

2nd Signal Squadron RE

Place	Date	Hour	Summary of Events and Information	Remarks and references to Appendices
	NOV.			
ST. SAUFLIEU	1st.	12 NOON	At 12 noon through to 5th Cav. Bde. on phone & morse, CONTY intermediate	FW
	2d	4.13pm	2d Cav. Bde at CREUSE put on phone VIA AMIENS	FW
		5pm	Oxford Hussars at ORESMAUX through by phone and morse our office intermediate 4th Cav Bde and Oxfords.	
	3rd		6th Dragoon Guards at NEUVILLE-SOUS-LOEUILLY intermediate our office and 5th Signal Troop at CONTRE. 2d Cavalry Divn. School at BUSSY-les-daours put on phone via AMIENS and CORBIE exchange	FW
	4th		Airline detachment completed work ~~for~~ for us and commenced on lines for 4th Army remaining attached to unit.	FW
	5th		4th Army cut our pair at DURY and are on our exchange	FW
	6th		2d Bde RHA at RUMIGNY put on phone. Through to 4th Army on morse	FW
	7th		Nothing to report.	FW
	8th		Usual routine	FW
	9th		Nothing to report.	FW
	10th		O.C. Signals Cavalry Corps visited Squadron	FW
	11th		Usual routine	FW

Instructions regarding War Diaries and Intelligence Summaries are contained in F. S. Regs., Part II. and the Staff Manual respectively. Title pages will be prepared in manuscript.

WAR DIARY
or
~~INTELLIGENCE SUMMARY~~.
(*Erase heading not required.*)

Army Form C. 2118.

2d Signal Squadron RE

Place	Date	Hour	Summary of Events and Information	Remarks and references to Appendices
	NOV			
ST-SAUFLIEU	12		All signallers. flag pair work in the morning, reading Lucas lamp in the afternoon 2/Lt R.B. Johnson IV Hsrs. and 2 ORs. for work on RHA line left and joined 2d Bde RHA	FW.
	13-16		Usual routine, visual signalling, cable to RHA at RUMIGNY picked up on 14th.	FW
	17		Mounted party and cyclists march at 1pm, billet at MERICOURT sur SOMME Signal Office closed at ST SAUFLIEU at 3pm, reopened MONCHY LAGACHE same hour, communication to Cavalry Corps at VILLERS CARBONNEL by morse and telephone	FW
MONCHY LAGACHE	18		Mounted party and cyclists march at 4pm to MONCHY LAGACHE communication to all Brigades by D.R. only	FW
"	19		Office closed except for telephone communication at 11pm V.B.R. opened at VILLERS FAUCON in 55th Dvn. Signal office same hour through to advanced Cavalry Corps at FINS at 11pm	FW.
	20		Office closed at VILLERS FAUCON. 2pm, report centre opened at GOUZEAUCOURT at 3 PM communication to Cavalry Corps by mounted D.R. and motor cyclist Divisional report centre moved to sunken road L.36.c.4.6. at 8pm cable laid to Canadian Brigade near MASNIERES. cyclists left at VILLERS-PLUICH	FW

T2134. Wt. W708—776. 500000. 4/15. Sir J. C. & S.

Army Form C. 2118.

Instructions regarding War Diaries and Intelligence Summaries are contained in F. S. Regs., Part II. and the Staff Manual respectively. Title pages will be prepared in manuscript.

~~WAR DIARY~~
WAR DIARY
~~INTELLIGENCE SUMMARY.~~
(Erase heading not required.)

2d Signal Squadron RE

Place	Date	Hour	Summary of Events and Information	Remarks and references to Appendices
	NOV			
	20		Advanced Cavalry Corps at MARCOING motor cyclists and car went on to MASNIERES	FW
	21		Communication to Brigades by mounted DR. Report centre moved back to VILLERS FAUCON at 5pm. communication through 55th Division to Cavalry Corps at FINS, motor cyclists etc. returned to VILLERS FAUCON	FW
	22		Signal office moved to FINS at 3pm Squadron marched at 5pm Lieut. MACINTYRE 20th Hussars evacuated sick to Base	FW
	23		Squadron moved to W.2.C.7.4. at 3pm Signal office opened there, and through to Cavalry Corps at FINS on morse and telephone	FW
	24		Moved to FLESQUIERES at 6.30 AM communication to Cavalry Corps by telegraph and telephone and by wireless, to Guards Division and 40th Division by telephone, report centre returned to W.2.C.7.4. at 4pm through to Corps by telephone 4th Cavalry Brigade took over Signal office at FLESQUIERES	FW
	25		Through to Corps by telegraph at 8AM	FW
	26		Stopped near DESSART WOOD	FW

Instructions regarding War Diaries and Intelligence Summaries are contained in F. S. Regs., Part II. and the Staff Manual respectively. Title pages will be prepared in manuscript.

WAR DIARY
or
~~INTELLIGENCE SUMMARY.~~
(Erase heading not required.)

2nd Signal Squadron RE

Army Form C. 2118.

Place	Date	Hour	Summary of Events and Information	Remarks and references to Appendices
	NOV			
FINS	27		Report centre moved over at 2pm and took over Corps Signal office at FINS Corps moved back to VILLERS CARBONNEL, communication to Corps morse and telephone also to 4th Corps, and to 5th Cav Bde who took over our old office at DESSART WOOD	[initials]
	28		"B" Echelon rejoined from MONCHY LAGACHE	[initials]
	29		Remained at FINS	
	30		Ordered up at 12.15pm 5th Cav Bde office taken over that hour Forward office opened at W.3.C.6.9 at 2.10pm through by telephone that hour and by morse at 2.50pm, visual to Brigades by Lucas lamp Squadron returned to FINS at ~~4~~ 4.30pm. (VBR.) Forward office remain open	[initials]
	~~31~~		~~Squadron parade 6.30AM and set at W.3.C.6.9 at 7AM, return to FINS at 4pm. Main trunk just outside signal office blown up by shell. Through by wireless both yesterday and today~~	

[initials]

Captain XI Hrs
Cmdg 2nd Signal Sqdn RE

T2134. Wt. W708—776. 500000. 4/15. Sir J. C. & S.

WO 95/29

Confidential

War Diary

of

2d Signal Squadron RE

From 1st December 1917

To 31st December 1917

Volume XL

Instructions regarding War Diaries and Intelligence Summaries are contained in F. S. Regs., Part II. and the Staff Manual respectively. Title pages will be prepared in manuscript.

WAR DIARY
or
~~INTELLIGENCE SUMMARY.~~
(Erase heading not required.)

Army Form C. 2118.

2nd Signal Squadron RE

Place	Date	Hour	Summary of Events and Information	Remarks and references to Appendices
	DEC.			
FINS	1		Squadron parade at 6.30AM and move to W.3.C.6.9. Headquarters remain at FINS squadron return there at 4PM. Main trunk just outside signal office blown up by a shell. Through by wireless. At 3pm office moved about 500 yards along sunken road S of main road owing to battery of 8" Hows being brought into action at W.3.c.6.9 office remained open all night	FW
	2		Squadron remain at FINS office staff only remain at W.3.C.6.9	FW
	3		As for 2d	FW
	4		Back route blown up by shell fire communication made good by borrowing spare lines from FINS - NURLU route. communication opened to Cavalry Corps forward office at VILLERS-FAUCON at 11pm also to 3d Cavalry Bde at FARM at who took over portion of the line in front of HEUDECOURT	FW
	5		At 2PM forward area heavily shelled all communication forward cut except ~~by~~ one pair to our advanced office and to FARM at 4.45pm all back communication cut by shell fire. Squadron evacuated huts and picket line owing to heavy shell fire	FW

T2134. Wt. W708—776. 500000. 4/15. Sir J. C. & S.

Instructions regarding War Diaries and Intelligence Summaries are contained in F. S. Regs., Part II. and the Staff Manual respectively. Title pages will be prepared in manuscript.

WAR DIARY

~~or~~

~~INTELLIGENCE SUMMARY.~~

(Erase heading not required.)

2nd Signal Squadron RE

Army Form C. 2118.

Place	Date	Hour	Summary of Events and Information	Remarks and references to Appendices
	DEC			
	6	9AM	Office closed at FINS and reopened CARTIGNY at 12 NOON only cmn by D.R. up to 4pm at that hour telephone through to 7th Corps at LE CATALET. Mounted party & cyclists left FINS 11AM arrive CARTIGNY 2.30pm	[initials]
	7		Office closed 9AM. Mounted party and cyclists march to BUSSY LES DAOURS All office staff under O.C. proceed direct to ST SAUFLIEU. Office opened there at 1pm through to Cavalry Corps at VILLERS CARBONNEL by morse and telephone and to AMIENS exchange by telephone At 4pm office staff ordered to move to QUEVAUVILLERS communication maintained at ST SAUFLIEU till 7PM owing to uncertainty of lines at new place ~~Ops~~ only communication at new place is by DR with the civil exchange as emergency.	[initials]
	8		Mounted party and cyclists march 9AM to QUEVAUVILLERS	[initials]
	9		At 11AM through to Cavalry Corps by telephone only via AMIENS exchange also to 3rd Cavalry Bde at CREUSE morse and telephone at same hour through to Cavalry Corps morse direct at 1 45pm. Locals G.S. & Q.	[initials]
	10		OC ASC and orderly room put on telephone	

T2134. Wt. W708—776. 500000. 4/15. Sir J. C. & S.

Instructions regarding War Diaries and Intelligence Summaries are contained in F. S. Regs., Part II. and the Staff Manual respectively. Title pages will be prepared in manuscript.

WAR DIARY
or
~~INTELLIGENCE SUMMARY.~~
(Erase heading not required.)

2nd Signal Squadron RE

Army Form C. 2118.

Place	Date	Hour	Summary of Events and Information	Remarks and references to Appendices
	DEC			
QUEVAUVILLERS	11		Through to 4th Cavalry Brigade on telephone only	FW
	12		Through to Supply column through SALEUX exchange and to 5th Cavalry Brigade on morse with 20th Hussars intermediate and by telephone via POIX and HORNOY civil exchanges	FW
	13		4th Cavalry Brigade put through on morse	FW
	14		Improving local circuits	FW
	15		Nothing to report	FW
	16		4th Cavalry Field Ambulance at NAMPS au VAL put on phone	FW
	17		Usual routine. DRLS. to 4th Cav Bde at COURCELLES by mounted DR	FW
	18		Morse set installed at POIX to take traffic for 169th Army Troops Artillery	FW
	19		nothing to report	FW
	20		Another morse set installed at POIX to transmit to 12th Lancers. personnel for Signals for Dismounted Bde. under Lt Codrington 16th Lancers. OC 5th Signal Troop left to take over line	FW
	21		Nothing to report	FW

T2134. Wt. W708–776. 500000. 4/15. Sir J. C. & S.

Instructions regarding War Diaries and Intelligence Summaries are contained in F. S. Regs., Part II. and the Staff Manual respectively. Title pages will be prepared in manuscript.

WAR DIARY

~~or~~

~~INTELLIGENCE~~ ~~SUMMARY.~~

(*Erase heading not required.*)

2d Signal Squadron RE

Army Form C. 2118.

Place	Date	Hour	Summary of Events and Information	Remarks and references to Appendices
	DEC			
QUEVAUVILLERS	22		Usual routine difficulty experienced with D.R. service on account of snow most runs are late	[initials]
	23		D.R.L.S. run by cars	[initials]
	24		-do-	[initials]
	25		Signal Office closed except for Priority work from 12 noon to 8 pm	[initials]
	26		D.R.L.S. by mounted D.R.	[initials]
	27		-"-	[initials]
	28		-"- Through to 6th D.Gs. at ~~[illegible]~~ NAMPS-AU-MONT by phone	[initials]
	29		Usual routine. Divisional school moved to DURY.	[initials]
	30		-"- Mounted DRs still employed for DRLS.	[initials]
	31		Divisional school at DURY put through by phone as temporary measure through 18th Corps Heavy Artillery exchange at DURY on to AMIENS ex. On 30th personnel for signals for Dis[illegible] Division changed Lieut H.A.T. Brand 12th R. Lcrs. O.C. 4th Signal Troop taking command	[initials]

[signature] Lieut for
O.C. 2d Signal Squadron RE

T2134. Wt. W708—776. 500000. 4/15. Sir J. C. & S.

Vol 30

Confidential

War diary

of

2d Signal Squadron RE

From 1/1/18 to 31/1/18

Vol No XLI

Instructions regarding War Diaries and Intelligence Summaries are contained in F. S. Regs., Part II. and the Staff Manual respectively. Title pages will be prepared in manuscript.

WAR DIARY
or
~~INTELLIGENCE~~ SUMMARY.
(Erase heading not required.)

Army Form C. 2118.

2nd Signal Squadron R.E.

Place	Date	Hour	Summary of Events and Information	Remarks and references to Appendices
	JAN 1918			
QUEVAUVILLERS	1		Usual routine. motor cyclist DRs commenced running one post each day at 2pm to all units. Visual signalling ie:- flag drill in afternoon	
	2		Usual routine. Flag drill etc.	
	3		-do- -do- OC visited 5th Signal Troop	
	4		line built to stores. OC visited 3d Signal Troop	
	5		Usual routine	
	6		OC visited Dismounted Division	
	7		line maintenance, usual routine	
	8		Usual routine OC visited AD Signals at CATALET	
	9		AD Signals visited Squadron and inspected offices, billets etc.	
			Lt. Ragnean Deccan Horse joined from Signals Cavalry Corps	
	10		Usual routine	
	11		Working party sent out to help 3d Cav Bde Sig Tp build line to 4th Hussars at PROUZEL	
	12		3d Hussars put through on telephone direct	
	13		Usual routine	

WAR DIARY
or
~~INTELLIGENCE SUMMARY~~.
(Erase heading not required.)

Army Form C. 2118.

Instructions regarding War Diaries and Intelligence Summaries are contained in F. S. Regs., Part II. and the Staff Manual respectively. Title pages will be prepared in manuscript.

2nd Signal Squadron RE

Place	Date 1918	Hour	Summary of Events and Information	Remarks and references to Appendices
	JAN			
QUEVAUVILLERS	14		Usual routine	FW
	15		nothing to report	FW
	16		A.D. Signals visited unit. Lieut Codrington 16th Lancers O.C. 5th Signal Troop handed over command of Troop to Lord Francis Hill R.S. Greys and proceeded to 1st Signal Squadron to take over command there.	FW
	17		O.C. visited Dismounted Division, Lieut Courtney RE 2d Signal Troop relieved Lieut Brand 12th Lancers, as O.C. Signals 2d Dismtd Bde	FW
	18		Nothing to report usual routine	FW
	19		Usual routine	FW
	20		-do-	
	21		Squadron parade mounted for individual exercises, drill etc	FW
	22		Usual routine Lamp signalling in afternoon	FW
	23		-do- -do-	FW
	24		-do- visual signalling in afternoon	FW
	25		-do- -do-	
	26		O.C. visited 4th Cavalry Divn Signals at ATHIES	

T2134. Wt. W708—776. 500000. 4/15. Sir J. C. & S.

Instructions regarding War Diaries and Intelligence Summaries are contained in F. S. Regs., Part II. and the Staff Manual respectively. Title pages will be prepared in manuscript.

WAR DIARY

~~or~~

~~INTELLIGENCE SUMMARY.~~ 2nd Signal Squadron R.E.

(Erase heading not required.)

Army Form C. 2118.

Place	Date 1918	Hour	Summary of Events and Information	Remarks and references to Appendices
	JAN			*
QUEVAUVILLERS	27		O.C 4th Signal Squadron came down from ATHIES to look at lines accommodation etc	[initials]
	28		Usual routine. part of personnel with Dismtd Div rejoined	[initials]
	29		-do- Remainder of Dismtd Div rejoined units	
	30		Nothing to report	[initials]
	31		Usual routine	[initials]

Lieut for [signature] Captain.
Cmdg. Signals, 2nd Cavalry Division.

T2134. Wt. W708–776. 500000. 4/15. Sir J. C. & S.

Vol 31

Confidential

War. Diary

Of

2nd Signal Squadron. R.E

FROM - Feb 1st 1918 TO. Feb 28th 1918

Vol. No XLII

Instructions regarding War Diaries and Intelligence Summaries are contained in F. S. Regs., Part II. and the Staff Manual respectively. Title pages will be prepared in manuscript.

WAR DIARY

~~INTELLIGENCE SUMMARY.~~

(*Erase heading not required.*)

Army Form C. 2118.

February 1918 — 2nd Signal Squadron RE

Place	Date	Hour	Summary of Events and Information	Remarks and references to Appendices
	FEB			
QUEVAUVILLERS	1		Usual routine	Vfw
	2		Advance party proceeded to ATHIES. 3rd Cav Bde closed down at CREUSE	Vfw
	3		Nothing to report	Vfw
	4		4th Cav Bde, 5th Cavalry Bde & 20th Hussars taken off morse and phone at 11.40 5th Cav Bde opened at CREUSE	Vfw
	5		5th Cav Bde. closed at CREUSE, reopened MARCELCAVE, 3rd Cav Bde opened at ST CHRIST. mounted portion & cyclists march to MARCELCAVE	Vfw
ATHIES	6		2nd Cavalry Divn closed at QUEVAUVILLERS at 11am reopened at ATHIES same hour, remainder of Squadron march to ATHIES 5th Cavalry Bde opened at ENNEMAIN	Vfw
	7		Nothing to report	Vfw
	8		4th Cavalry Brigade opened at DEVISE	Vfw
	9		Nothing to report	Vfw
	10		Usual routine	Vfw
	11		—do—	Vfw.

T2134. Wt. W708—776. 500000. 4/15. Sir J. C. & S.

Instructions regarding War Diaries and Intelligence Summaries are contained in F. S. Regs., Part II. and the Staff Manual respectively. Title pages will be prepared in manuscript.

Army Form C. 2118.

WAR DIARY

~~or~~

~~INTELLIGENCE~~ ~~SUMMARY~~.

(Erase heading not required.) 2d Signal Squadron RE

Place	Date	Hour	Summary of Events and Information	Remarks and references to Appendices
	FEB			
ATHIES	12		Nothing to report usual routine	[illegible]
	13–19		-do- -do-	[illegible]
	20		-do- -do-	[illegible]
	21		-do- "	
	22		" "	
	23		" "	
	24		" "	
	25		Re Regulating and Strengthening of Brigade Routes - Started	[illegible]
	26		-do- -do-	[illegible]
	27		" "	[illegible]
	28		" "	

[illegible signature]

Captain.

Cmdg. Signals, 2nd Cavalry Division.

T2134. Wt. W708–776. 500000. 4/15. Sir J. C. & S.

No 32

Confidential

War Diary of

2nd Signal Squadron R.E.

From 1/3/18 To 31/3/18

Vol. No XLIII

Instructions regarding War Diaries and Intelligence Summaries are contained in F. S. Regs., Part II. and the Staff Manual respectively. Title pages will be prepared in manuscript.

Army Form C. 2118.

WAR DIARY
or
~~INTELLIGENCE SUMMARY.~~
(Erase heading not required.)

March 1918 — 2nd Signal Squadron RE

Place	Date	Hour	Summary of Events and Information	Remarks and references to Appendices
	MARCH			
ATHIES	1		4th Cavalry Brigade moved from DEVISE to ATHIES. Oxfordshire Hsrs, 4th M.G.S. + 9th M.V.S. in communication VIA 5th Cav Bde. 3d Hsrs + 6th D.Gs through 3rd Cav Bde. communication established with 17th I.B. at MONTECOURT by phone at 1.5pm and by morse at 1.45pm also by morse + phone with 72nd I.B. at DEVISE	[illegible]
	2		72nd I.B. est. communication direct with 24th Div and taken off V.B. exchange	[illegible]
	3		Usual routine	[illegible]
	4		Nothing to report	[illegible]
	5		3d Cavalry Bde closed at ST-CHRIST and proceeded to VERMAND. 5th Lancers took over their old office	[illegible]
	6-8		Nothing to report usual routine	[illegible]
	9		Cavalry Corps closed at CATELET reopened at VILLERS CARBONNEL 19th Corps taking over at CATELET through to them on morse + phone	[illegible]
	10	5.15pm	Communication est with Cavalry Corps and 3d Cav Div direct	[illegible]
	11		3d Cav Bde returned from VERMAND to ST CHRIST and took over old office	[illegible]

Instructions regarding War Diaries and Intelligence Summaries are contained in F. S. Regs., Part II. and the Staff Manual respectively. Title pages will be prepared in manuscript.

WAR DIARY
or
~~INTELLIGENCE SUMMARY.~~
(Erase heading not required.)

2nd Signal Squadron RE.

Army Form C. 2118.

Place	Date	Hour	Summary of Events and Information	Remarks and references to Appendices
	MARCH			
ATHIES	12		5th Cav Bde taken off morse, still in communication by phone	
	13		Three Brigades closed down and moved to new area, our office closed at 11AM and handed over to 3rd Cav Div. Office reopened	
		11 AM	at QUESMY same hour in communication with 3rd Corps	
QUESMY		4.30pm	through to 5th Cav Bde in QUESMY Captain FV Drake XI Hussars handed over command of Squadron to Lieut AC Macintyre XX Hrs and proceeded to Cavalry Corps to take over tempy. command of the Cavalry Corps Signal Squadron	
	14		Communication on phone & morse est with 3rd & 4th Cav Bdes at GRANDRU, usual locals	
	15		Improving local circuits	
	16-19		Usual routine, nothing to report	
	20	3pm	3rd Bde RHA moved to X17.d.7.1 sheet 66D. communication via 3rd Corps and VILLERQUIER-AU-MONT	
	21		All Brigades furnish dismtd. party, personnel sent from unit to 3rd Corps, and to 3rd Signal Troop to assist owing to pressure of work	

Instructions regarding War Diaries and Intelligence Summaries are contained in F. S. Regs., Part II. and the Staff Manual respectively. Title pages will be prepared in manuscript.

WAR DIARY
or
~~INTELLIGENCE~~ SUMMARY.
(*Erase heading not required.*)

2d Signal Squadron R.E.

Army Form C. 2118.

Place	Date	Hour	Summary of Events and Information	Remarks and references to Appendices
	MARCH			
QUESMY	22		3d & 4th Cav. Bdes put through on new lines - Army route 4 & 7	ACML
	23	4pm	Office closed at QUESMY and handed over to 9th French Division, new office opened at PONTOISE no communication by wire. on 22d. Lt Macintyre 4 motor cyclists & 3 linemen proceeded with G.O.C. to 14th Division. 4 mounted D.Rs. to ~~XIX~~ III Corps for duty	ACML
	24.		~~Cpl Bellar~~ Cpl Cook motor cyclist doing duty with 14th Division wounded while carrying dispatches near Guiry and evacuated. motor bicycle captured by enemy. Office closed at PONTOISE at 2PM reopened BAILLY 6pm. no communication except by D.R.	ACML
	25		Office closed BAILLY at 9.30AM, reopened PONTOISE at 10.15AM closed at PONTOISE 7.30pm and reopened CHIRY 10pm communication to French Infy Divn by phone at CHIRY and to 3rd Corps at RIBECOURT and 14th Div. at CHIRY	ACML
	26		Division moved to DIVE-LE-FRANC sheet 70E 34.A.8.6. (V.B.R.) advanced Office opened there at 11.15AM closed & returned to CHIRY at 11.50PM through on French military by phone through RIBECOURT to III Corps for priority calls only	ACML

T2134. Wt. W708–776. 500000. 4/15. Sir J. C. & S.

Instructions regarding War Diaries and Intelligence Summaries are contained in F. S. Regs., Part II. and the Staff Manual respectively. Title pages will be prepared in manuscript.

WAR DIARY
~~or~~
~~INTELLIGENCE~~ SUMMARY.

(Erase heading not required.) 2nd Signal Squadron R.E.

Army Form C. 2118.

Place	Date	Hour	Summary of Events and Information	Remarks and references to Appendices
	MARCH			
CHIRY	27		Office closed at CHIRY at 10 AM and reopened at VENETTE at 3 PM. O.C. rejoined unit at VENETTE. Office closed at 5.30pm and reopened at JONQUIERES 6.30pm. Sapper Filtness and Driver Ware wounded by high explosive shell on CHIRY - RIBECOURT road 2 horses also Killed	ACM
	28		Office closed JONQUIERES at 6.15 AM report centre opened at X roads 1 mile SW of CERNOY at 8.20 AM closed at 8.55 AM, reopened at MONTGERAIN 10 AM closed at 12 noon, opened at CHEPOIX 2.30pm closed 4.30pm, opened ANSAUVILLERS 5.15pm communication only by DR	ACM
	29		Office closed at ANSAUVILLERS 2.10pm reopened at BOVES 6.45pm under XIX Corps through by phone through BOVES exchange at 9pm	ACM
	30		Advance office opened at GENTELLES at 9 AM through on phone to advanced 61st Divn. office and to advanced 19th Corps on phone at 11.58 AM. Lines were Dis twice during the day for an hour through shell fire	ACM.
	31		Mounted party joined adv office at GENTELLES lines continually blown up by shell fire	ACM

A. W. MacIntyre
Captain.
Comdg. Signals, 2nd Cavalry Division.

T2134. Wt. W708–776. 500000. 4/15. Sir J. C. & S.

Vol 33

Confidential

War Diary

of

2nd Signal Squadron R.E.

From 1/4/18 To 30/4/18

Vol. No XLIV

Instructions regarding War Diaries and Intelligence Summaries are contained in F. S. Regs., Part II. and the Staff Manual respectively. Title pages will be prepared in manuscript.

WAR DIARY
or
~~INTELLIGENCE SUMMARY.~~
(Erase heading not required.)

Army Form C. 2118.

April 1918. 2nd Signal Squadron RE

Place	Date	Hour	Summary of Events and Information	Remarks and references to Appendices
	APRIL			
	1		At 12 midnight 31st March 1st April the division was ordered to retake the BOIS DE HANGARD. Attack was launched at 9AM. The following communication was arranged. A line was laid from GENTELLES (Adv Div. H.Q.) to battle H.Q: at ruined house on main AMIENS - ST QUENTIN road N of DOMART by 9AM Another line was laid by LT TUCZEK Essex Yeomanry from there to General SEELY'S H.Q. at HANGARD; both lines were through and working by 9AM. Later about an hour after the attack began the line was blown to pieces and repaired time after time by various linemen of the Division. Sapper S. CLARKE showed great gallantry in doing this When divisional H.Q. was shelled the line to GENTELLES was broken in 18 places in 300 yards. This was repaired and put through by Sapper D. BUTLER under continuous shell fire along the road. Visual communication was established with 4th Cav Bde.	
			The attack met with great success, and communications were very satisfactory considering the heavy shell fire. At 8pm battle H.Qrs closed and the General staff returned to GENTELLES.	ACW

T2134. Wt. W708—776. 500000. 4/15. Sir J. C. & S.

Instructions regarding War Diaries and Intelligence Summaries are contained in F. S. Regs., Part II. and the Staff Manual respectively. Title pages will be prepared in manuscript.

WAR DIARY
or
~~INTELLIGENCE SUMMARY.~~
(*Erase heading not required.*)

2d Signal Squadron RE

Army Form C. 2118.

Place	Date	Hour	Summary of Events and Information	Remarks and references to Appendices
	APRIL			
GENTELLES	2		Squadron moved back to BOYES at 11 AM leaving advanced ~~HQ~~ Office open which closed at GENTELLES at 6.30pm.	acuu.
BOYES	3		Office closed at BOYES at 11 AM and reopened same hour at RIVERY	
RIVERY			working telephone to Cavalry Corps at that hour, through by noon at 12.35pm	acuu
	4		At 12.10pm unable to get Cavalry Corps large shell dropped on route and broke up all lines, through and working OK at 2.8pm.	acuu.
	5		Cavalry Corps line very earthy owing to route being damaged by shelling	acuu.
	6		Office closed at RIVERY at 11 AM. Mounted party moved 6AM. Office	
	~~8~~		reopened at AILLY-le-haut-Clocher at 2pm. communication to Brigades by D.R only. Locals GS & Q. VB office intermediate on Cavalry Corps – Abbeville M.O.	acuu
	7		Improving local circuits	acuu
	8-9		Nothing to report	acuu
	10		Office closed at AILLY at 4pm reopened at AUXI-LE-CHATEAU at 6pm in same office as used by Cavalry Corps and 1st Cavalry Division	
	11		Standing too under 1 hours notice	acuu

T2134. Wt. W708–776. 500000. 4/15. Sir J. C. & S.

Instructions regarding War Diaries and Intelligence Summaries are contained in F. S. Regs., Part II. and the Staff Manual respectively. Title pages will be prepared in manuscript.

WAR DIARY
or
~~INTELLIGENCE SUMMARY.~~
(Erase heading not required.)

2d Signal Squadron RE

Army Form C. 2118.

Place	Date	Hour	Summary of Events and Information	Remarks and references to Appendices
	APRIL			
AUXI-LE-CHATEAU	12		Advanced Divl. HQ moved to FRUGES arrive 3pm and await orders. signal office at Auxi closes that hour. At 5pm move to BOMY office opened at 7.30pm through to Cavalry Corps 7.30pm on morse and telephone	[illegible]
	13		Office closed at BOMY and reopened at BLARINGHEM at 1.30pm. on phone to 15th Corps at B.8.a.8.6. and 1st Australian Div. at SIRCUS. At 7pm through to Cavalry Corps at MOULIN-LECOMTE on phone and morse	[illegible]
	14		Advanced Divl. H.Q. moved to Grand HASARD office opened 8AM and through to SIRCUS exchange manned by our personnel, thence to V.B. at BLARINGHEM mounted party remain at SIRCUS till 4pm the return to BLARINGHEM advanced office closed and returned 7pm. Wireless wagon broke down on way up to Gd HASARD and was replaced by new wireless section from Cavalry Corps by 12 noon	[illegible]
	15		Mounted party remain in billets at BLARINGHEM. Advanced Div. HQ re-established at Gd HASARD at 8AM, through on morse and phone to Cavalry Corps & 2d Cav Div, on phone to 1st Australians, 3rd Cavalry Bde. at Bois-des-huit-rues, 4th Cavalry Bde at SIRCUS, 5th CaBde at Gd HASARD	[illegible]

T2134. Wt. W708—776. 500000. 4/15. Sir J. C. & S.

Instructions regarding War Diaries and Intelligence Summaries are contained in F. S. Regs., Part II. and the Staff Manual respectively. Title pages will be prepared in manuscript.

WAR DIARY
or
~~INTELLIGENCE~~ SUMMARY.
(Erase heading not required.)

Army Form C. 2118.

2d Signal Squadron RE

Place	Date	Hour	Summary of Events and Information	Remarks and references to Appendices
	APRIL		(Cont)	
BLARINGHEM	15		Office remained open all night. Adv HQ return to BLARINGHEM	
	16		At 12.30pm Advanced office closed at Gd HASARD. At 3pm telegraph comn established with 15th Corps. our office intermediate Cav Corps + 15th Corps. 5th Cavalry Brigade at BLARINGHEM put on phone also 3d Cav Bde at LYNDE and 4th Cav Bde at SIRCUS remain on	acwl
	17		Immediate award of M.M. to 38756 Cpl motor cyclist R.C. Robinson, 23487 Sapper S. Clarke and 7037 Sapper D Butler	acwl.
	18		Improving local circuits	acwl
	19		Nothing to report OC visited A.D. Signals Cav Corps for conference	acwl
	20		Usual routine	acwl
	21-23		Nothing to report	acwl
	24		3d Cavalry Brigade return to LYNDE from EECKE	acwl
	25-26		Usual routine	acwl
	27		3d Cavalry Brigade at 8AM close at LYNDE and reopen same hour at HEURINGHEM communication morse and phone to 2d Army at BLENDECQUES. 4th Cavalry Brigade close at SERCUS at 8AM reopens	

T2134. Wt. W708—776. 500000. 4/15. Sir J. C. & S.

Instructions regarding War Diaries and Intelligence Summaries are contained in F. S. Regs., Part II. and the Staff Manual respectively. Title pages will be prepared in manuscript.

WAR DIARY or ~~INTELLIGENCE SUMMARY~~.

(*Erase heading not required.*)

Army Form C. 2118.

2d Signal Squadron RE

Place	Date	Hour	Summary of Events and Information	Remarks and references to Appendices
	APRIL			
BLARINGHEM	27		same hour at LYNDE communication morse + phone direct 3d Hussars take over SERCUS exchange	[initials]
	28		Usual routine, nothing to report	[initials]
	29		At 12 noon office closes at BLARINGHEM and reopens same hour at COYECQUE communication by morse + phone to Cavalry Corps and 3d Cavalry Division, our office intermediate	[initials]
	30		Improving local circuits	[initials]

[signature] Captain
Cmdg 2d Signal Squadron RE

Vol 34

CONFIDENTIAL

War Diary of

2nd Signal Squadron. R.E.

From 1st May 1918 To 31st May 1918

Vol. No XLV

Instructions regarding War Diaries and Intelligence Summaries are contained in F. S. Regs., Part II. and the Staff Manual respectively. Title pages will be prepared in manuscript.

WAR DIARY
or
~~INTELLIGENCE SUMMARY.~~
(Erase heading not required.)

Army Form C. 2118.

May 1918 — 2nd Signal Squadron R.E.

Place	Date	Hour	Summary of Events and Information	Remarks and references to Appendices
	MAY			
COYECQUE	1		Usual routine, nothing to report	ACM
	2-3		-do- -do-	ACM
	4		3rd Cavalry Division taken out of circuit	ACM
	5		Office closed at COYECQUE at 11 AM reopened at MONTCAVREL same hour communication through civil exchange to G.H.Q. thence to Cavalry Corps, at 3.55 pm through to G.H.Q. on morse and phone, at 9.45 pm G.H.Q. put us through direct to 3rd Army on phone and direct to Cavalry Corps on morse	ACM
	6		Communication with 3rd Cavalry Bde at LEFAUX via ETAPLES exchange	ACM
	7		3rd Bde RHA at MONTESCHORE chateau put on our exchange. 4th Cavalry Brigade at RECQUES on morse and phone	ACM
	8		5th Cavalry Brigade at AIX-en-ISSART put through on morse & phone and 2nd Field Squadron R.E. on phone at ALETTE	ACM
	9-10		Nothing to report	ACM
	11		A.S.C. at ALETTE put on phone. Captain V HUME 9th Lancers	ACM

T2134. Wt. W708—776. 500000. 4/15. Sir J. C. & S.

Instructions regarding War Diaries and Intelligence Summaries are contained in F. S. Regs., Part II. and the Staff Manual respectively. Title pages will be prepared in manuscript.

WAR DIARY
or
~~INTELLIGENCE SUMMARY.~~
(Erase heading not required.) 2d Signal Squadron RE

Army Form C. 2118.

Place	Date	Hour	Summary of Events and Information	Remarks and references to Appendices
	MAY			
MONTCAVREL	11		temporarily attached from Cavalry Corps Signals	ACM
	12		Nothing to report	ACM
	13		Lecture given by MAJOR JAMES MC. RAF to all Signalling officers of Division. Capt. V. HUME 9th Lancers returned to Cavalry Corps	ACM
	14		Cable to 5th Cav. Bde. replaced by pole route	ACM
	15–23		Nothing to report	ACM
	24		– do –	ACM
	25		G.O.C. Division inspected the Squadron in marching order	ACM
	26–30		Nothing to report	ACM
	31		– do –	ACM

ACM [signature] Captain
Cmdg 2d Signal Sqdn RE

T2134. Wt. W708—776. 500000. 4/15. Sir J. C. & S.

To G.S.

W.D. 35

Confidential

War diary
of

2nd Signal Squadron R.E.

From 1-6-18

To 30-6-18

Vol. No XLVI

Instructions regarding War Diaries and Intelligence Summaries are contained in F. S. Regs., Part II. and the Staff Manual respectively. Title pages will be prepared in manuscript.

WAR DIARY

~~or~~

~~INTELLIGENCE SUMMARY.~~

(Erase heading not required.)

Army Form C. 2118.

2nd Signal Squadron R.E.

Place	Date	Hour	Summary of Events and Information	Remarks and references to Appendices
MONTCAVREL.	June 1st		Usual routine. Canteen opened.	[initials]
"	2nd		Usual routine.	[initials]
"	3rd		G.S.O.1's office put on separate line	[initials]
"	4th		P.E.L. lorry returned from Abbeville with new engine.	[initials]
"	5th		Usual routine.	[initials]
"	6th		Usual routine.	[initials]
"	7th		Usual routine.	[initials]
"	8th		Squadron Marching order parade. Section prizes for best turn-out won by The Richardson's (20th Hussars) section. Judged by Major Kerans M.C. and Capt Hall M.C.	[initials]
"	9th		Church Parade.	[initials]
"	10th		Battalion of American Infantry marched through billets in morning.	[initials]
	11th		Scheme with 6 Sqdn R.A.F using new POPHAM panel. The scheme proved an unqualified success.	[initials]
	12th		Nothing to report.	[initials]

T2134. Wt. W708—776. 500000. 4/15. Sir J. C. & S.

Instructions regarding War Diaries and Intelligence Summaries are contained in F. S. Regs., Part II. and the Staff Manual respectively. Title pages will be prepared in manuscript.

WAR DIARY
or
INTELLIGENCE SUMMARY.
(Erase heading not required.)

Army Form C. 2118.

Place	Date	Hour	Summary of Events and Information	Remarks and references to Appendices
Montcavrel	13th		Concert given by Concert Party from Hesdin. Very largely attended.	ACM
"	14th		Nothing to report usual routine.	ACM
"	15th		Nothing to report usual routine. Squadron Parade 2.30 pm.	ACM
"	16th		Church Parade for C of E.	ACM
"	17th		Nothing to report. Usual routine.	ACM
"	18th		Usual routine.	ACM
"	19th		Usual routine.	ACM
"	20th		Gas demonstration by D. G. O. riding through gas cloud of chlorine. Box respirators worn by all ranks for ½ hour.	ACM
"	21st		Nothing to report. Usual routine.	ACM
"	22nd		Squadron parade 2.30 pm and Gas Drill.	ACM
"	23rd		Wireless section inspected by O.C. Wireless Cavalry Corps. Billets where P.U.O. (Influenza) cases were billetted sprayed out by 4a Sanitary Section. Isolation tent erected	ACM

Instructions regarding War Diaries and Intelligence Summaries are contained in F. S. Regs., Part II. and the Staff Manual respectively. Title pages will be prepared in manuscript.

WAR DIARY
or
INTELLIGENCE SUMMARY.
(Erase heading not required.)

Army Form C. 2118.

Place	Date 1918	Hour	Summary of Events and Information	Remarks and references to Appendices
MONTCAVREL	June 24		Cable Telephone circuit to 3rd Bde. RHA replaced by "Air Line" and extended to a pair of lines allotted by G.H.Q. on the NEUVILLE sous MONTREUIL — FRUGES route as far as CLENLEU thus obtaining communication between 4th Cav Bde and 6th Dragoon Guards, through this office. Telephonic through our exchange, on morse we become "intermediate".	WAS
	25		Usual Routine: 2/Cpl. Eyre. R.E. Spr Judd & Cpl. Herbert R.E. awarded M.S.M. London Gazette 17/6/18	WAS
	26		Usual Routine	WAS
	27		Box Respirators (Anti-Gas) worn by all ranks for half an hour.	WAS
	28		Usual Routine: Sgt. Egan. 20 Hussars. Sgt M/C Partridge R.E. Corpl. M/C Cook R.E. and 2/Cpl Westlake R.E. interviewed by Major Gen. T.T. Pitman. C.B., C.M.G., who presented them with cards stating his appreciation of their services during the war.	WAS
	29		Squadron Parade 11 am for inspection of Arms. Equipt. Iron Rations and Gas Drill	WAS
	30		Usual Routine.	WAS

W A Lucas ? Lieut
Essex Yeomanry
for Captain,
Cmdg. Signals, 2nd Cavalry Division.

T2134. Wt. W708—776. 500000. 4/15. Sir J. C. & S.

WO 95/1136

CONFIDENTIAL

War Diary of

2nd Signal Squadron R.E.

From. 1 - 7 - 18
TO. 31 - 7 - 18

VOLUME No. XLVII.

Instructions regarding War Diaries and Intelligence Summaries are contained in F. S. Regs., Part II. and the Staff Manual respectively. Title pages will be prepared in manuscript.

WAR DIARY
or
~~INTELLIGENCE SUMMARY~~.
(Erase heading not required.)

Army Form C. 2118.

2nd Signal Squadron RE

Place	Date	Hour	Summary of Events and Information	Remarks and references to Appendices
	July			
MONTCAVREL	1st		Usual Routine: General Parade 9pm for reading ~~order~~ of Sections 4 – 44 of the Army Act in accordance with Para 461 Kings Rules & Regulations.	~~WAT~~
			The 3rd Bde Hd Qrs moved from ~~Lefaux~~ LEFAUX to ROSOMEL CHATEAU one mile South of FRENCQ. Communication between the Bde and ETAPLES closed down at 3pm and reopened same hour via SAMER–BOULOGNE and G.H.Q.	WAT
	2nd		O.C. Line visited 4th and 3rd Bdes Signal Troops and reconnoitred a route for a direct telephone circuit between the two Brigades with a view to getting more direct communication to the 3rd Bde. Indented on GHQ for necessary Stores.	WAT
	3rd		Usual Routine,	WAT
	4		Usual Routine, All ranks wore Box Respirators for half an hour. Commenced building line to 3rd Bde.	WAT
	5		Usual Routine. Continued building line to 3rd Bde; Capt A.C. Macintyre	
	~~6~~		~~Usual Routine~~ rejoined from Hospital	WAT
	6		Usual Routine. Squadron Parade at 11 am for Inspection of all arms and "Gas Drill".	

T2134. Wt. W708—776. 500000. 4/15. Sir J. C. & S.

Instructions regarding War Diaries and Intelligence Summaries are contained in F. S. Regs., Part II. and the Staff Manual respectively. Title pages will be prepared in manuscript.

WAR DIARY
or
~~INTELLIGENCE SUMMARY.~~
(Erase heading not required.)

Army Form C. 2118.

2nd Signal Squadron R.E.

Place	Date	Hour	Summary of Events and Information	Remarks and references to Appendices
	July			
MONTCARREL.	7th		Usual routine. Line construction to 3rd Cav. Bde.	ACM
—	8th		Usual routine. Line construction to 3rd Cav Bde.	ACM
—	9th		Nothing to report. Line construction as above	ACM
—	10th		Nothing to report. Line construction as above.	ACM
—	11th		Inspection of 5th Brigade Signal Troop by O.C.	
—			Signals. Line construction as above	ACM
—	12th		Usual Routine	ACM
—	13th		Usual Routine, Squadron Parade Weekly Inspection of all Arms. Divn Under Orders to Move	ACM
WAIL	14th		Division moved to WAIL, Communications, CAR by Phone, ZCO on horse, A.D. Cable Section joined from Cavalry Corps. No 7 Wireless Pack rejoined Cavalry Corps. No 4 Pack joined this Unit temporarily.	ACM
LE CAUROY	15		Division moved to Le CAUROY. Communication with RCO, YCO. and PD. by Telegh Lines, on Phone	ACM
—	16		Nothing to Report, Connected up local offices to Exchange.	ACM
	17		PC moved to EPS.	ACM
	18		Usual Routine	ACM

T2134. Wt. W708—776. 500000. 4/15. Sir J. C. & S.

Instructions regarding War Diaries and Intelligence Summaries are contained in F. S. Regs., Part II. and the Staff Manual respectively. Title pages will be prepared in manuscript.

WAR DIARY
or
~~INTELLIGENCE SUMMARY~~.
(*Erase heading not required.*)

Army Form C. 2118.

2nd Signal Squadron R.E.

Place	Date	Hour	Summary of Events and Information	Remarks and references to Appendices
LE CAUROY	July 19th		Usual Routine.	ACM
"	20		Lines to CAO on Morse + Phone PE Intermediate	ACM
"	21		Usual Routine. Supply Col on Phone.	ACM
WAIL	22.		Division moved to WAIL Comms to CAR + YCO.	ACM
MONTCAVREL	23		Divn moved to MONTCAVREL. CAR phone, YCO morse, PD + PE on Morse + Phone.	ACM
"	24.		Usual Routine, Strengthening and Staying of Lines in the Area.	ACM
"	25		Usual Routine. Lieut C H Vignoles rejoined A D Cable Section from leave.	ACM
	26		Usual Routine, Line Maintenance, Etc.	ACM
	27.		" " Squadron Parade Weekly Inspection of all Arms.	ACM
	28.		Nothing to Report, Usual Routine	ACM
	29		Nothing to Report, " " Cable line built from Montcavrel to Recques	ACM
	30		" " "	ACM
	31		Nothing to Report, " " No 4 Wireless Pack to Cav Corps viz No 7 Pack from Wireless Squadron Cav Corps to this unit	ACM

A C McCaintyre (?)
Captain.
Cmdg. Signals, 2nd Cavalry Division.

T2134. Wt. W708—776. 500000. 4/15. Sir J. C. & S.

WD 37

Confidential

War Diary

2nd Signal Squadron R.E.

From 1-8-18

To 31-8-18

Volume No XLVIII

Instructions regarding War Diaries and Intelligence Summaries are contained in F. S. Regs., Part II. and the Staff Manual respectively. Title pages will be prepared in manuscript.

WAR DIARY
or
INTELLIGENCE SUMMARY.
(Erase heading not required.)

Army Form C. 2118.

2nd Signal Squadron RE

Place	Date	Hour	Summary of Events and Information	Remarks and references to Appendices
MONTCAVREL	August 1.		~~Nothing to report~~. Construction of new cct. to RECQUES by AD Cable section. 4th Cav. Bde to ST JOSSE telephone on D.G.T. [illegible]	WAS
	2.		~~Nothing to report~~. Signal office re-wired. Cable cct. replaced by open wire.	WAS
	3.		Nothing to report. Later. Order to move received 7 pm.	WAS
	4		Division moved at 9pm to TORTEFONTAIN. The mounted section marched under 2Lt CR Jennings OXFORD Hussars arriving TORTEFONTAIN 4 am 5th inst. Divisional Report Centre closed at MONTCAVREL at 9pm opening TORTEFONTAIN same hour. Comm by telephone and morse to Cavalry Corps by 9.10 pm arriving there at 2AM 6 inst	WAS
	5th		The mounted Section marched to CAOURS. [illegible] miles N.E. of ABBEVILLE. Remainder of Squadron remained at TORTEFONTAIN. ~~at~~ Comm same as for 4th.	WAS
	6th		Nothing to report	WAS
	7		Divisional Report Centre closed at TORTEFONTAIN and reopened at BRAILLY at 8am. The mounted Section having left CAOURS the night previous arrived at BRAILLY at 5AM. At 11pm the whole of squadron less B. Echelon and the P.E.L Lorry marched to LONGEAU arriving at 3am on the 8inst. Communication by telephone through PICQUINY and AILLY to Cavalry Corps advanced but on morse also.	WAS

T2134. Wt. W708—776. 500000. 4/15. Sir J. C. & S.

Instructions regarding War Diaries and Intelligence Summaries are contained in F. S. Regs., Part II. and the Staff Manual respectively. Title pages will be prepared in manuscript.

WAR DIARY
or
~~INTELLIGENCE~~ SUMMARY.
(Erase heading not required.)

Army Form C. 2118.

2nd Signal Squadron RE

Place	Date	Hour	Summary of Events and Information	Remarks and references to Appendices
LONGEAU	8th		3 am Communication established with Cavalry Corps. in the Same Village by runners and mounted orderly.	WAF
		9am	Report centre moved to N32C 5.3 near CACHY. Communication obtained by telephone and motorcyclist Despatch Rider.	
		10AM	Report centre moved to ORCHARD north of CACHY, advanced Cavalry Corps Head Quarters established at the Same place	
		1pm	Report centre opened at V13 C55. Ref Map 62D 1/40000	
		2.30pm	Report Centre moved to W30 C 8.5 Ref map 62D 1/40000	
		5pm	Report centre moved to E13 D 1.8 " " "	
		9.15pm	Report Centre opened at W30 C 8.5 . " " N.W. of CAIX where the Squadron remained till dawn 9th inst.	
	9th	5am	Head Quarters moved to E8 B8.8. Telephonic communication obtained with Cavalry Corps by joining on to the 1st Cav Div line	WAF
		5pm	Divisional Report Centre moved to E30 A 3.7 (Reference map 66E) NW of WARVILLERS where it remained till following morning. Wireless ~~and~~ Telephonic and Telegraphic communication obtained to Cavalry Corps. Wireless to 3rd Cavalry Bde. Remainder of Division by Despatch Rider.	

T2134. Wt. W708—776. 500000. 4/15. Sir J. C. & S.

Instructions regarding War Diaries and Intelligence Summaries are contained in F. S. Regs., Part II. and the Staff Manual respectively. Title pages will be prepared in manuscript.

WAR DIARY
or
~~INTELLIGENCE~~ SUMMARY.
(Erase heading not required.)

Army Form C. 2118.

2d Signal Squadron RE

Place	Date	Hour	Summary of Events and Information	Remarks and references to Appendices
NW of WARVILLERS	10/8/18	~~11am~~ 8.30am	Div Report Centre opened at D5B6.9 S.W. of CAYEUX. Telephonic ~~&telegraphic~~ was communication established with Cavalry Corps situated in same Village	
		1pm	Division moved forward through WARVILLERS to a position NE of the Village. During the advance under orders of the AD Signals Cavalry Corps the Cable head of the 3rd Cav Div at BEAUFORT WOOD was picked up and carried on by the AD Cable section to a point SE of ROUVROY where Divisional Head Quarters were expected to go to. As the Head Quarters did not ~~f~~ move up to this point the line was continued to the NE ~~edge~~ of the Village and handed over to the Head Quarters of the 1/5 Border Regt and split at WARVILLERS thus giving communication to Cavalry Corps (rear half) and one of the leading Infantry Battalions (front half) for Liaison purposes	
		4pm	Wireless erected & communication obtained with Cavalry Corps & 3rd Cav Bde	
		~~5~~	About 5pm Divisional Head Quarters moved back to E17C1.9 about	
		9.30pm	1 mile SE of CAIX. Communication Established by telephone & telegraph with Cavalry Corps. Wireless erected at the point and communication Established with 3 Bde ~~and~~ Cavalry Corps also.	

T2134. Wt. W708—776. 500000. 4/15. Sir J. C. & S.

Instructions regarding War Diaries and Intelligence Summaries are contained in F. S. Regs., Part II. and the Staff Manual respectively. Title pages will be prepared in manuscript.

WAR DIARY
or
INTELLIGENCE SUMMARY.
(Erase heading not required.)

Army Form C. 2118.

2nd Signal Squadron RE

Place	Date	Hour	Summary of Events and Information	Remarks and references to Appendices
	10/8/18		Throughout the day several Air Reconnaissance reports were dropped by No 6 Squadron. Intercommunication between Cavalry & Aircraft proving quite successful.	WAS
	11/8/18, 12/8/18, 13/8/18, 14/8/18		Remained at E17C1.9. Communications improved by replacing cable with airline. The lines were broken intermittently by hostile bombing, but were quickly repaired. Messages dealt with on the 13th inst 215. On the 14th inst 200.	WAS
	15/8	12noon	Report Centre closed at E17C1.9 and reopened at BELLOY-sur-SOMME at 12noon. Communication with Cavalry Corps by Telephone and Telegraph VIA. PICQUINY	
	16/8		Nothing to report. 2Lt VIGNOLES A.D.CABLE Section evacuated sick to Cavalry Field Ambulance.	WAS
	17/8		Divisional Report Centre closed at BELLOY and reopened at FONTAIN-L'ETALON. Communication to Cavalry Corps by telephone and telegraph	WAS
	18/8		Communication established with all Brigades & the Division	WAS
	19/8		ADVS, DADOS, ADMS and MT Coy 2nd Cav Div put into Telephonic Communication. All Signal Officers attended a Conference held by AD Signals	WAS

T2134. Wt. W708—776. 500000. 4/15. Sir J. C. & S.

Instructions regarding War Diaries and Intelligence Summaries are contained in F. S. Regs., Part II. and the Staff Manual respectively. Title pages will be prepared in manuscript.

WAR DIARY
or
~~INTELLIGENCE SUMMARY.~~
(Erase heading not required.)

Army Form C. 2118.

2nd Signal Squadron R.E.

Place	Date	Hour	Summary of Events and Information	Remarks and references to Appendices
	19/8	10AM	Cavalry Corps at 10 am.	WAY
	20/8.		Most of the day spent collecting technical stores and distributing to Bde Signal Troops	WAY
	21/8		Capt. A.C. MacIntyre evacuated to ~~CCS~~ No 2B Casualty Clearing Station, Lt W.A. Tucker Essex Yeomanry took over command of the Squadron. Lt C.R. Jennings who was about to proceed to England on leave gave up the vacancy to proceed with the Division which was under orders to move forward, at two hours notice.	WAY
		9pm	At 9 pm the mounted Sections and "A D" Cable Section moved to GRENAS 5 miles N E of DOULLENS. S.S.M. WEEKS. M.M. rejoined the Sqdn from leave	
	22/8	8AM	Divisional Report Centre closed at FONTAIN L'ETALON and reopened at GRENAS same hour. Communication established with 3rd Army. 6th Corps. and all Cavalry Brigades by telephone, 5th Cav Bde & 3rd Army by telegraph.	WAY
		3pm	At 3 pm O.C. Signal Squadron ~~attended~~ a conference with D.D. Signals 3rd Army. At which it was decided to extend a line running from 3rd Army to POMMIER towards X 9 (Ref MAP 51.C.) by L16 Air Line Section Commanded by Lieut Turner R.E., and attach "AA" Cable section to the 2nd Signal Squadron for the purpose of maintaining communication	

Instructions regarding War Diaries and Intelligence Summaries are contained in F. S. Regs., Part II. and the Staff Manual respectively. Title pages will be prepared in manuscript.

WAR DIARY
or
INTELLIGENCE SUMMARY.
(Erase heading not required.)

Army Form C. 2118.

Place	Date	Hour	Summary of Events and Information	Remarks and references to Appendices
	22nd		communication between the 3rd Army and 2 Cav Div. when on the move. The cable so laid to be replaced by the L16 Airline Section with open wires as soon as possible after each bound. No 120 H.D. Mobile Pigeon Loft was placed at the disposal of the Division. Eight birds were drawn for the Division and Six for the 5th Cavalry Bde. The above arrangements were made in view of the advanced Divisional Report centre opening at X 9C 2.8, on 23rd inst at 6am vide 2nd Cav Div Order. No66 dated 22nd Aug 18. The 5th Cav Bde Report Centre ~~opens~~ to open at the same place and time. (6 am 23rd inst) The 3rd and 4th Cav Bdes remained at COULLEMENT and HUMBERCOURT respectively and Divisional Rear Head Quarters at GRENAS. The 3rd Bde RHA moved to WANINCOURT-LEZ-PAS and took over communications of 5th Cavalry Bde.	DAY
		8.30pm	No 4 Wireless Pack Set arrived from Cavalry Corps to be attached to a Bde as reqd. No 8 W Pack set having already been sent direct to 5th Cav Bde.	
		9.30pm	In accordance with verbal instruction received from G.S.O.1., arrangements for communication with two Brigades, 5th as before & 3rd at F 3C 9.1, with Divisional advanced Report Centre at W 30 a 8.1 were to be made	
		10pm	Orders issued for A.D. Cable Section, No.7 and No 4 Wireless Pack Sets, and remainder of mounted Personnel to march at 11pm under Lt C.R. Jennings. O.X.Y. to W30.a 8.1 with the following instructions. At Daybreak 23rd inst One Cable wagon under Sgt Sughrue	

T2134. Wt. W708—776. 500000. 4/15. Sir J. C. & S.

Instructions regarding War Diaries and Intelligence Summaries are contained in F. S. Regs., Part II. and the Staff Manual respectively. Title pages will be prepared in manuscript.

WAR DIARY
or
INTELLIGENCE SUMMARY.
(Erase heading not required.)

Army Form C. 2118.

[illegible] Signal Squadron RE

Place	Date	Hour	Summary of Events and Information	Remarks and references to Appendices
	22/8/18	10pm	to lay a cable pair from W30a8.1 (near MONCHY au BOIS) to X9c2.8 (EAST of RANSART) the other waggon under Lt CR Jennings to lay a telephone pair to F3c9.1 (West of DOUCHY.) Both of these line were completed by 6AM 23rd. The remainder	WAA
	23/8		of the mounted Section to remain at W30a8.1. About 3 am a party was sent out to intercept L 16 Airline Section and to direct them towards W30a8.1 which was working outwards from POMERA. Eventually the Situation necessitating the Divisional Advanced Report Centre moving to X9c.2.8 ~~and but~~ and communication to be arranged as previously ordered. At 5.30am the line run by Sgt Saghrue's section was handed over to the 6th Corps Advanced Exchange pending the arrival of L 16 Airline Section or the AA Cable Section with the 3rd Army line. At 6am Communication was established with the 3rd Army through the 6th Corps. Wireless Comm with the pack set attached to 5 Cav Bde to 3rd Army established at the same time. Lt Sale for ~~the~~ wireless Cavalry Corps having arrived about 1am took over the wireless Communication of the Division	WAA
		8.30am	Direct Line from CAR to Division established giving two outlets. This line	

T2134. Wt. W708—776. 500000. 4/15. Sir J. C. & S.

Instructions regarding War Diaries and Intelligence Summaries are contained in F. S. Regs., Part II. and the Staff Manual respectively. Title pages will be prepared in manuscript.

WAR DIARY
or
INTELLIGENCE SUMMARY.
(Erase heading not required.)

Army Form C. 2118.

2nd Signal Squadron RE

Place	Date	Hour	Summary of Events and Information	Remarks and references to Appendices
	23/8/18	8.35pm	superimposed with morse. Lieut Brown RE arrived from 3rd Army to join AD Cable Section. 5th Cavalry Bde moved forward to X17C5.6 Visual & W/T Comn established. Only a few messages were sent by Visual owing to difficulty afforded by the clouds of dust caused by moving columns of our troops. At 12.45 pm. Line run out to 5th Signals Bde by AD Cable Section at 3pm Div Head Quarters moved up to this point X17C5.6 At 6pm Report Centre moved to F3C9.1 (West of DOUCHY) Communication obtained without delay by taking up cable pair already laid in the early morning to this point & joining the end at W30A8.1 on to CAR Line, cutting out the portion going towards RANSART. During the day many messages were dropped by aeroplane. Two Brigades were in Communication by wireless except when actually moving. All rear units in telephonic or telegraphic communication through 3rd Army or 6th Corps. The number of messages dealt with throughout the day was 212.	WAT
	24/8	9am	AD Cable Section left to run a line to 3rd Cav Bde at MOYENNEVILLE	WAT
		9.30am	Div Report Centre moves to F6C.8.8 (Sheet 57D) present report centre becoming intermediate until ~~now~~ Telephone line superimposed with morse. The intermediate Station closed down at 10.42am	

T2134. Wt. W708—776. 500000. 4/15. Sir J. C. & S.

WAR DIARY
or
INTELLIGENCE SUMMARY.
(Erase heading not required.)

Army Form C. 2118.

Instructions regarding War Diaries and Intelligence Summaries are contained in F. S. Regs., Part II. and the Staff Manual respectively. Title pages will be prepared in manuscript.

2d Signal Squadron RE

Place	Date	Hour	Summary of Events and Information	Remarks and references to Appendices
	24/8	12.45pm	Report Centre again moved to A3d7.9 West of MOYENNEVILLE. Communication established to 4th Cav Bde & 3rd Cav Bde by telephone. 3rd and 5th Cav Bdes & 3rd Army by wireless, to 3rd Army by telephone and morse. Telephone communication was interrupted for about one hour through one leg of the circuit to the 3rd Army being broken, well behind, around MONCHY. This was attended to by Army linemen directly the fault was localised. Telegraphic communication was maintained throughout without any interruption. About 5pm Report Centre moved back to ~~A3d7.9~~ F2a2.9 (West of DOUCHY.) Communication by telephone and morse to 3rd Army. Telephone to 3rd Cavalry Bde. By wireless to 5 Cav Bde and 3rd Army. 4 Cav Bde ~~by~~ D.R. At this point we remained for the night. Throughout the day many messages were dropped by aeroplanes and messages sent on POPHAM Panel to aircraft. The number of messages dealt with throughout the day was. 389	WdL
	25/8	8am	Divisional Report Centre closed at F2a2.9 and reopened at GRENAS at the same hour. As Brigades returned to the same area before the Division	WdL

T2134. Wt. W708—776. 500000. 4/15. Sir J. C. & S.

Instructions regarding War Diaries and Intelligence Summaries are contained in F. S. Regs., Part II. and the Staff Manual respectively. Title pages will be prepared in manuscript.

WAR DIARY
or
INTELLIGENCE SUMMARY.
(Erase heading not required.)

Army Form C. 2118.

Place	Date	Hour	Summary of Events and Information	Remarks and references to Appendices
	25.		moved on 23rd. The original circuits that were in use were taken over again.	WAL
	26		In a state of readiness to move at 2 hours notice. until further orders.	WAL
	27		Horse Inspection, Gas mask Inspection.	WAL
	28		Local offices put on telephone ASC. ADMS	WAL
	29		Communication established by telephone to 3rd Bde RHA GUADIEMPRE through MONDICOURT. PAS and HENU	WAL
	30		Motor Cycle Inspection. Push Cycle inspection, Ordinary Routine	WAL
	31.		Horse inspection by OC. otherwise nothing to report.	WAL

W A Lucas [illegible] Lieut, Cmdg 2nd Signal Sqdn R.E.

Pass Summary

T2134. Wt. W708—776. 500000. 4/15. Sir J. C. & S.

Confidential

War diary

of

2nd Signal Squadron R.E.

From. 1-9-18 to 30-9-18

Vol. No. XL[illegible]IX

Instructions regarding War Diaries and Intelligence Summaries are contained in F. S. Regs., Part II. and the Staff Manual respectively. Title pages will be prepared in manuscript.

WAR DIARY
or
~~INTELLIGENCE SUMMARY.~~
(*Erase heading not required.*)

Army Form C. 2118.

2d. Signal Squadron R.E.

Place	Date 1918 Hour		Summary of Events and Information	Remarks and references to Appendices
	Sept			
GRENAS	1/9/18		Squadron still at 2 hours notice to move., nothing to report.	WAY
	2nd/9		nothing to report. The 1 Kilowatt PEL Set attached to Division Exchange for a 3 Kilowatt Wireless Set. Cpl D.R. Cooke V rejoins from Base Hospital	WAY
	3/9		Division becomes GHQ reserve, and comes under four hours notice to move	
		2 pm	5 Cavalry Bde moves to PAS. Communication by Spletting line to 3rd Bde RHA at GUADIEMPRE and putting RHA on 5th Cavalry Bde Exchange. 12 Lancers moves to WARLENCOURT. Communication through to 5th Cavalry Bde by picking up original line of the Bde to Division. The Division becoming intermediate	WAY
	4/9		nothing to report.	WAY
	5/9		nothing to report.	WAY
	6/9		5th Cav Bde and 3rd Cav Bde come under 4th and 1st Armies respectively	WAY
			No 4 Wireless Pack set withdrawn from 3rd Cav Bde and with No 7 Pack Set sent to Cavalry Corps	WAY
	7/9		One M/C DR and two Visual Signallers attached to each Bde 3rd Bde RHA and 3rd Field Sqdn R.E. in telephonic communication at FAMIECHON	WAY

T2134. Wt. W708—776. 500000. 4/15. Sir J. C. & S.

Instructions regarding War Diaries and Intelligence Summaries are contained in F. S. Regs., Part II. and the Staff Manual respectively. Title pages will be prepared in manuscript.

WAR DIARY
or
~~INTELLIGENCE SUMMARY.~~
(Erase heading not required.)

Army Form C. 2118.

2nd Signal Squadron RE

Place	Date	Hour	Summary of Events and Information	Remarks and references to Appendices
GRENAS	8/9/18		Nothing to report. Lt C R Jennings to England on leave	WAY
	9/9/18		2Lt Rea. 4th Hussars temporarily attached returns to his Regt. for duty	WAY
	10/9/18		Nothing to Report.	
	11/9/18		Mounted Sections moved to CAUMESNIL into billets, A.S.C. moved to MONDICOURT.	WAY
	12/9/18		Weekly Inspection of Gas masks. Also worn by all ranks for half an hour. ASC put on telephone at MONDICOURT.	WAY
	13/9/18		Nothing to Report	WAY
	14/9/18		Nothing to Report	WAY
	15/9/18		A D Cable Section under 2/Lt W D Brown marched to 3rd Cav Div to be temporarily attached.	WAY
	16/9/18		Nothing to Report.	WAY
	17/9/18		Nothing to report	WAY
	18/9/18		Squadron Parade Inspection of Arms Equipt &c.	WAY
	19/9/18		A D Cable Section rejoined	WAY
	20/9/18		Nothing to report	WAY
	21/9/18		Nothing to report.	WAY

Instructions regarding War Diaries and Intelligence Summaries are contained in F. S. Regs., Part II. and the Staff Manual respectively. Title pages will be prepared in manuscript.

WAR DIARY
or
INTELLIGENCE SUMMARY.
(Erase heading not required.)

2nd Signal Squadron R.E.

Army Form C. 2118.

Place	Date	Hour	Summary of Events and Information	Remarks and references to Appendices
GRENAS	22/9/16		A D Cable Section moved to join the 3rd Signal Sqdn.	WAT
	23/9		Nothing to report.	WAT
	24/		Nothing to report.	WAT
	25/		Nothing to report	WAT
	26		Arms & Equipment Inspection. Nothing else to report.	WAT
	27.		Motor & Push bicycle inspection. Capt Truzek to England on leave. 2nd Lt C R Jenning commdg Sqdn during Capt Truzek's absence. Z.C.P. moved forward 8 pm and ceased direct d.r.'s service. circulation through 4th army also 5th bde.	CJ
	28		nothing to report	CJ
	29		Church Parade 10 am nothing further to report.	CJ
	30		Course commenced in elementary telephony for Divisional Observation Sect.	CJ

C R Jenning Lieut.
~~Captain.~~
Cmdg. Signals, 2ND Cavalry Division.

T2134. Wt. W708—776. 500000. 4/15. Sir J. C. & S.

Vol 39

Confidential

War diary

of

2nd Signal Squadron R.E.

From 1-10-18

To 31-10-18

Vol. No. L

Instructions regarding War Diaries and Intelligence Summaries are contained in F. S. Regs., Part II. and the Staff Manual respectively. Title pages will be prepared in manuscript.

October 18.

WAR DIARY
or
~~INTELLIGENCE SUMMARY.~~
(Erase heading not required.)

Army Form C. 2118.

2nd Signal Squadron R.E.

Place	Date	Hour	Summary of Events and Information	Remarks and references to Appendices
	October			
GRENAS	1		Nothing to report	CRJ
	2		Saddle Inspection 15.00 nothing else to report	CRJ
	3		Weekly arms etc inspection and pay parade. Dismounted party GRENAS 09.50 Mounted Party CAUMESNIL 10.50 Containers of all box respirators in use before 1/1/1918 were changed under supervision of Divisional Gas N.C.O.	CRJ
	4		~~Official intimation received that TURKEY had surrendered unconditionally and hostilities had ceased~~. Nothing further to report	CRJ
	5		4th Bde rept centre closed HUMBERCOURT 09.00 reopened PAS same hour. Telephone and telegraph were opened at 11.00 by splitting line to 3rd Bde RHA and Field Squadron at GUADIEMPRE and putting latter 2 office on 4th Bde exchange	CRJ
	6.		Church Parade 10.00 Inspection of billets GRENAS 11.30 stables & billets CAUMESNIL 12.00.	CRJ
	7		Visual Signallers Parade 09.00 Scheme 09.00 to 11.15	CRJ
	8/10		Nothing to report	CRJ

D. D. & L., London, E.C.
(A8004) Wt W1771/M2031 750,000 5/17 Sch. 52 Forms/C2118/14

Army Form C. 2118.

Instructions regarding War Diaries and Intelligence Summaries are contained in F. S. Regs., Part II. and the Staff Manual respectively. Title pages will be prepared in manuscript.

WAR DIARY
or
~~INTELLIGENCE SUMMARY.~~
(Erase heading not required.)

2nd Signal Squadron RE

Place	Date	Hour	Summary of Events and Information	Remarks and references to Appendices
	October			
GRENAS	11th / 19th		Nothing to report.	WAY
	20th		3rd Army move to MESNIERS, 5pm. Conn arranged by C.A.R. and necessary changes made by them. Line from 4th Cav Bde to 3rd Army; old H.Q.rs later onto DOULLENS EXCHANGE giving second outlet to Cav Corps via 4th ~~Bde~~ Cav Bde, DOULLENS – AMIENS – 4th Army –	WAY
	21st / 27th		Nothing to report. Usual daily routine.	WAY
	~~28~~		Usual routine	
	29		4th Cav Bde Head Quarters moved to CAUDRY nine miles SE of CAMBRAI. Line to PAS joined through to GUADIEMPRE giving 3rd Bde RHA and 3rd Field Squadron. Line to DOULLENS exchange changed over and brought into the office on Route running from PAS – MONDICOURT – GRENAS. GOC 2 Cav Div inspected the horses of the Squadron.	WAY
	~~29~~ 30		Nothing to report.	WAY
	31		Nothing to report.	WAY

W A Lucas(?) Captain.
Cmdg. Signals, 2ND Cavalry Division.

D. D. & L., London, E.C.
(A8504) Wt W1771/M2031 750,000 5/17 Sch. 52 Forms/C2118/14

40

Confidential

War Diary

of

2d Signal Squadron RE

From 1/11/18

To 30/11/18

Vol No LI

Instructions regarding War Diaries and Intelligence Summaries are contained in F. S. Regs., Part II. and the Staff Manual respectively. Title pages will be prepared in manuscript.

WAR DIARY

~~or~~

~~INTELLIGENCE SUMMARY.~~

(*Erase heading not required.*)

Army Form C. 2118.

2nd Signal Squadron R.E.

Place	Date Nov	Hour	Summary of Events and Information	Remarks and references to Appendices
GRENAS.	1.		Nothing to report.	WAY
do	2		- do -	WAY
do	3.		- do -	WAY
do	4		- do -	WAY
do.	5.		- do -	WAY
do.	6.		Mounted Party of Squadron marched to BAPAUME en route to CAMBRAI.	WAY
CAMBRAI	7		Report centre closed at GRENAS and opened at CAMBRAI. Communication established to Cavalry Corps via 3rd Army 5th Cavalry Bde via 3rd Army, 4th Army and 9th Corps. 4th Cav Bde and 3rd Cav Bde via 3rd Army	
do	8		Nothing to report.	WAY
do	9		- do -	} WAY
do	10		- do -	
do.	11		- do -	
do.	12.		- do -	WAY
do	13.		Mounted party left for BOUSSIES en route for MAUBEUGE.	WAY
do	14		Nothing to report.	
MAUBEUGE	15.		Report centre closed at CAMBRAI and reopened MAUBEUGE. 12 noon, Communication established via 6th Corps at MAUBEUGE.	WAY
do.	16.		A D Cable Section rejoined from 3rd Cav Div. Nos 7 and 4 Wireless Pack sets joined from Cavalry Corps.	WAY

D. D. & L., London, E.C.
(A8004) Wt W1771/M2031 750,000 5/17 Sch. 52 Forms/C2118/14

Army Form C. 2118.

Instructions regarding War Diaries and Intelligence Summaries are contained in F. S. Regs., Part II. and the Staff Manual respectively. Title pages will be prepared in manuscript.

WAR DIARY

~~or~~

~~INTELLIGENCE SUMMARY.~~

(Erase heading not required.)

Place	Date	Hour	Summary of Events and Information	Remarks and references to Appendices
MAUBEUGE	17.		Div Head Qrs closed MAUBEUGE reopened THUIN.	WAL
THUIN	18.	1400	Report centre closed THUIN, reopened MORIALME same hour. Communication by Wireless to 5th Cav Bde and 4th Army	WAL
MORIALME.	19		Nothing to report	WAL
do	20		-do-	WAL
	21	1200	Report centre closed MORIALME and reopened BOUVIGNES, same hour. Communication as on the 18th.	WAL
BOUVIGNES	22	1200	Report centre closed at BOUVIGNES reopened at LEIGNON same hour. Telephone cmn obtained with 3rd Cav Bde at CINY Remainder by wireless.	WAL
LEIGNON	23.		Report centre moved to Marche opening 1200	WAL
MARCHE	24		Telephonic Cmn established to Adv. 6th Corps. Remainder of Cmn by wireless.	WAL
do	25		Nothing to report	WAL
do	26.		Telephonic Cmn established to 5th Cav Bde, and 2 telephone circuits obtained to 9th Corps.	WAL
do	27.		Nothing to report.	WAL
do	28		-do-	WAL
do	29		No 7 Pack Set (Wireless Telegraph) transferred to 1st Cav Div.	WAL
do	30.		Nothing to report.	WAL

W A Lee [signature] Captain,
Cmdg. Signals, 2nd Cavalry Division.

D. D. & L., London, E.C. (A8004) Wt W1771/M2031 750,000 5/17 Sch. 52 Forms/C2118/14

Confidential

War Diary of

2d Signal Squadron RE

From 1/12/18 to 31/12/18

Vol. No LII

Instructions regarding War Diaries and Intelligence Summaries are contained in F. S. Regs., Part II. and the Staff Manual respectively. Title pages will be prepared in manuscript.

WAR DIARY
or
INTELLIGENCE SUMMARY.
(Erase heading not required.)

3rd Signal Squadron R.E.

Army Form C. 2118.

Place	Date	Hour	Summary of Events and Information	Remarks and references to Appendices
MARCHE	1st to 6th		Nothing to report	[illegible]
MARCHE	7th to 14th		Nothing to report.	
do	15th		Mounted party marched to BOMAL en route for THEUX.	
do	16th	noon	Office closed at Marche reopened Theux same hour. Through on Morse and Phone to Cavalry Corps. On phone to 3rd and 4th Cavalry Brigades. Wireless to 5th Cavalry Bdes.	[illegible]
THEUX.	17th		Wireless communication to 4th and 6th Cavalry Bdes. Communication to 3rd Cav Bde, by DRLS only.	
"	18th		— do —	
"	19th		— do —	
"	20th		3rd Cav Bde in Telegraphic and Telephonic communication Cmn to 4th and 5th Cav Bdes by wireless.	
"	21st to 23rd		— do — Making good German Tele routes for cmn to 4th Cav Bde	
"	24th		Cmn to 4th Cav Bde by Morse and phone.	
"	25th	1030	Office closed Xmas day	
	26th	730	Office reopened.	

D. D. & L., London, E.C. (A8004) Wt W1771/M2031 750,000 5/17 Sch. 52 Forms/C2118/14

Instructions regarding War Diaries and Intelligence Summaries are contained in F. S. Regs., Part II. and the Staff Manual respectively. Title pages will be prepared in manuscript.

Army Form C. 2118.

WAR DIARY
or
~~INTELLIGENCE~~ SUMMARY.
(Erase heading not required.)

2d Signal Squadron RE

Place	Date DEC	Hour	Summary of Events and Information	Remarks and references to Appendices
THEUX	27 to 31		Nothing to report	

Capt.
Cmdg. Signals, 2ND Cavalry Division.

D. D. & L., London, E.C.
(A8004) Wt W1771/M2031 750,000 5/17 Sch. 52 Forms/C2118/14

Vol 43

Confidential

War Diary

of

3rd Signal Squadron RE

From 1st to 28th February 1919

Volume LIV

Instructions regarding War Diaries and Intelligence Summaries are contained in F. S. Regs., Part II. and the Staff Manual respectively. Title pages will be prepared in manuscript.

Feb 1919.

WAR DIARY
or
~~INTELLIGENCE SUMMARY~~.

(Erase heading not required.)

2nd Signal Squadron R.E.

Army Form C. 2118.

Place	Date FEB	Hour	Summary of Events and Information	Remarks and references to Appendices
THEUX	1st to 7th		Nothing to report	[illegible]
	8th			
	9th		Lt. P. Hickens. Q.O.O.H. (attached) leave to U.K. 9.2.19	[illegible]
	10th to 14th		Nothing to report.	
	15th to 21st			[illegible]
	22nd to 25th			
	26th		Lt. C. R. Jennings. R.E. rejoined from leave from U.K. 26.2.19	[illegible]
			Lt. J. C. H. Jennings. D.C.M. R.E. on leave to U.K. from 26.2.19	[illegible]
	27th 28th		Nothing to report	[illegible]

[illegible] Capt 20th Hussars
Comdg 2nd Signal Squadron R.E.

D. D. & L., London, E.C.
(A8204) Wt W1771/M2031 750,000 5/17 Sch. 52 Forms/C2118/14

CONFIDENTIAL.

WAR DIARY

of

2nd signal Sqdn. R.E.

From. 1/3/19 to 31/3/19

(Volume LV.)

9/8

44

Army Form C. 2118.

Instructions regarding War Diaries and Intelligence Summaries are contained in F. S. Regs., Part II. and the Staff Manual respectively. Title pages will be prepared in manuscript.

WAR DIARY
or
~~INTELLIGENCE~~ SUMMARY.
(*Erase heading not required.*)

2nd Signal Squadron RE

Place	Date MARCH	Hour	Summary of Events and Information	Remarks and references to Appendices
THEUX	1st to 6th 7th		Nothing to report	GJ
	8th		A.D. Cable Section transferred from 2nd Signal Squadron to 2nd Corps	GJ
	9th		Nothing to report.	GJ
	10th	noon	Office closed at Theux reopened Heusy same hour. Communication with Corps, 3rd, 4th & 5th Brigades and other units by means of Civic Routes through Bureau Centrale, Verviers.	GJ
HEUSY. (VERVIERS)	11th to 18th		Nothing to report.	GJ
	19th		Lieut G.B.L. Jennings D.C.M. RE rejoined from leave to UK.	
	20th to 23rd		Nothing to report.	GJ
	24th		Lieut C.R. Jennings Oxford Hussars, left to command 7th Sig Tp RE	
	25th		G/296/30 received stating that 2nd Cavalry Division will cease to exist 31/3/19.	
	26th to 30th		Nothing to report.	GJ

G J Jennings Lt RE
Cmdg 2nd Signal Sqdn RE

D. D. & L., London, E.C.
(A8004) Wt W1771/M2031 750,000 5/17 Sch. 52 Forms/C2118/14

Confidential

War Diary

of

2nd Signal Squadron R.E.

From 1/4/19 to 30/4/19

Volume LVII.

Instructions regarding War Diaries and Intelligence Summaries are contained in F. S. Regs., Part II. and the Staff Manual respectively. Title pages will be prepared in manuscript.

WAR DIARY
or
~~INTELLIGENCE SUMMARY.~~
(Erase heading not required.)

2nd Signal Sqdn. R.E.

Army Form C. 2118.

Place	Date	Hour	Summary of Events and Information	Remarks and references to Appendices
HEUSY. (VERVIERS	April 1st to April 22nd		Nothing to report. Communications as in MARCH.	JAKT.
"	April 23rd	–	Lieut J.A.K. TAYLOR. 6th Res. Cav. Regt joined as ATTACHED from Cav. Corps Sig Sqdn. Cavalry Corps Signal Sqdn ceased to exist.	JAKT. JAKT.
"	April 24th			JAKT.
"	25th to 27th		Nothing to report.	
"	28th.		CAPT A.C. MACINTYRE leave to U.K. Lt J.A.K. TAYLOR commanding.	JAKT
"	29th 30th.		Nothing to report.	

J.A.K. Taylor
Lieut.
Cmdg
2nd Signal Sqdn R.E.

D. D. & L., London, E.C.
(A8004) Wt W1771/M2031 750,000 5/17 Sch. 52 Forms/C2118/14

www.ingramcontent.com/pod-product-compliance
Lightning Source LLC
Chambersburg PA
CBHW082009220426
43670CB00014B/2584